Small Moments: Personal Narrative Writing

DEDICATION

To Anna Marie Carrillo, the leader of P.S. 116, in appreciation for creating a school that demonstrates what's possible for every student.

FirstHand
An imprint of Heinemann
A division of Reed Elsevier Inc.
361 Hanover Street
Portsmouth, NH 03801-3912
www.heinemann.com

Offices and agents throughout the world

Copyright © 2003 by Lucy Calkins and Abby Oxenhorn

Photography: Peter Cunningham

The author and publisher wish to thank those who have generously given permission to reprint borrowed material:

Excerpt from *A Chair for My Mother* by Vera B. Williams. Copyright ©1982 by Vera B. Williams. Published by Greenwillow Books. Used by permission of HarperCollins Publishers.

Excerpt from *The Kissing Hand* by Audrey Penn. Published by Child and Family Press, an imprint of the Child Welfare League of America, Inc. (1993). Used by permission of the Child Welfare League of America, Inc.

Rubrics and checklists adapted by permission from *New Standards*. The *New Standards*® assessment system includes performance standards with performance descriptions, student work samples and commentaries, on-demand examinations, and a portfolio system. For more information, contact the National Center on Education and the Economy, 202-783-3668 or www.ncee.org.

Library of Congress Cataloging-in-Publication Data

Calkins, Lucy McCormick.
    Small moments : personal narrative writing / Lucy Calkins and Abby Oxenhorn.
    p. cm. — (Units of study for primary writing ; 2)
    ISBN 0-325-00528-1 (pbk. : alk. paper)
    1. English language-Composition and exercises-Study and teaching (Primary)--United States. 2. Narration (Rhetoric)--Study and teaching (Primary)--United States. 3. Autobiography-Authorship-Study and teaching (Primary)--United States-United States. 4. Curriculum planning-United States. I. Oxenhorn, Abby. II. Title.
    LB1529.U5C357 2003
    372.62'3--dc22   2003019531

Printed in the United States of America on acid-free paper

07   06   05   ML   4   5

SERIES COMPONENTS

▶ **The Nuts and Bolts of Teaching Writing** provides a comprehensive overview of the processes and structures of the primary writing workshop.

▶ You'll use **The Conferring Handbook** as you work with individual students to identify and address specific writing issues.

▶ The seven **Units of Study**, each covering approximately four weeks of instruction, give you the strategies, lesson plans, and tools you'll need to teach writing to your students in powerful, lasting ways. Presented sequentially, the Units take your children from oral and pictorial story telling, through emergent and into fluent writing.

▶ To support your writing program, the **Resources for Primary Writers CD-ROM** provides video and print resources. You'll find clips of the authors teaching some of the lessons, booklists, supplementary material, **reproducibles** and **overheads**.

SMALL MOMENTS: PERSONAL NARRATIVE WRITING

When my colleagues and I first began planning this yearlong curriculum, we asked ourselves, "Are there a few units of study that can work together to take children to the heart of what it means to write and live in a community of writers?" It soon became clear that for us, there was no question but that the school year must begin with us helping children understand that they can create stories out of the details of their own experiences.

Why This Unit?

Stories are so crucial to a child's language development that Gordon Wells, who performed a longitudinal study of twenty children and their language development throughout their school-aged years, concluded that of all the activities that were found to be characteristic of literate homes, the sharing of stories gave some children the most essential advantage. He concluded, "Constructing stories in the mind—or *storying*, as it has been called—is one of the most fundamental means of making meaning" (201).[1]

Although parents sometimes work to be sure their sons and daughters come to school knowing their colors, numbers, and ABCs, what in fact matters most to a child's later literacy are the opportunities children have to take the moments of their lives and spin them into stories. The average American parent talks with his or her child for only ten minutes a day. More and more children come to school unaccustomed to telling or hearing stories. A vast percentage of children arrive home after a day at school only to plug themselves into the television, the Game Boy, the VCR, or the computer. "Our children," Bill Moyers has said, "are being raised by appliances." Sitting among children at snack time, we listen in on their talk and notice that most of it is functional conversation. "I want that." "Pass the napkin." "Move over." "I was sitting there." Very little of this talk involves reminiscing or retelling the events of their lives. This unit of study is important in that it helps us create, in our classrooms, a culture of storytelling, positioning children to see their lives as full of stories!

Because stories are so crucial to a child's literacy development, this unit has become especially significant to all the co-authors of this series. If our children are going to be at home with literacy, they need to read, write, and talk the language that creates new worlds ("One time my dad and me went to the park. It was sunny. We looked and looked for . . .), as well as the language that works inside the existing world ("I want that one"). For us, this unit is not only about storytelling, but is also about the sort of responsive listening that can lead us to gasp in empathy and to laugh in delight at each other's stories.

About This Unit

Before Abby Oxenhorn (a talented kindergarten teacher), my colleagues, and I could begin to plan a unit on *Small Moments*, we needed to clarify the genre we would be teaching our children to write. Some people use the terms *memoir* and *personal narrative* interchangeably and confuse both with *realistic fiction*. Although we didn't plan to tell kindergartners the working definitions we'd settle on for each genre, we decided that it would help if we arrived at a consensus about what each of these genre

---

[1] *The Meaning Makers: Children Learning Language and Using Language to Learn.* Gordon Wells, Heinemann, 1986.

entailed. What follows is what we decided. For some common examples of each genre, turn to your CD-ROM.

> ▸ **Personal narratives** are chronological stories about one's life: this happens, then this, then this. They contain characters (the central character will be the author), a plot (two or more events occur in a sequence of time), and they take place in a setting. The plot usually involves a problem that is solved, a tension that is resolved, or something big that changes.

> ▸ In a **memoir**, an author tries to say something important about himself or herself. The memoir says, "This was the best moment of my childhood" or "My love of music made me who I am today." Memoirs often contain one or more personal narratives, but they may be structured as lists rather than as stories. Always, they contain an element of reflection.

> ▸ **Realistic fiction** contains the elements of story. The text may or may not be true; either way, it unfolds in continuous events and the reader enters into the world of the story, experiencing it as it happens.

Memoir	Realistic Fiction	Personal Narrative
Chicken Sunday Patricia Polacco	A Chair for My Mother Vera B. Williams	Salt Hands Jane Chelsea Aragon
Just Us Women Jeannette Franklin Caines	Owl Moon Jane Yolen	Do Like Kyla Angela Johnson
The Two of Them Aliki	Fireflies Julie Brinckloe	Joshua's Night Whispers Angela Johnson
When I Was Young in the Mountains Cynthia Rylant	The Kissing Hand Audrey Penn	Night Shift Daddy Eileen Spinelli
Shortcut Donald Crews	The Snowy Day Ezra Jack Keats	I Fly Anne Rockwell

Two discoveries informed the shape of this unit. First, we found it wasn't easy to locate *published* examples of personal narratives written for children because by the time a personal narrative reaches the printing press, the author has usually developed it into a story or a memoir. For example, *Owl Moon* began as Jane Yolen's account of her husband's many expeditions into the woods with their sons to search for an owl, but before it was published, it became realistic fiction. Julie Brinkloe's *Fireflies* reads as a personal narrative, but it, too, is realistic fiction.

Second, we realized that the stories our children love as readers tend to be much longer than those they could ever write. Published authors can write about broad expanses of time without sacrificing detail. *Owl Moon*, for example, tells of a child's entire evening and yet Yolen includes details such as the crunch of footsteps in snow. If a six-year-old tried to chronicle his entire evening, his text would be an underdeveloped list of events.

Because our goal is to teach youngsters to retell a sequence of events with precise detail, and to write in such a way that a reader could follow those events, we decided that in this unit we would not conduct a traditional genre study, say, of personal narrative writing. Instead, we decided to set children up to write very focused vignettes—what we call Small Moments—from their lives. For the purpose of this *Small Moments* unit, we decided that we'd sometimes use snippets of fictional stories, as well as of personal narratives or memoirs as exemplars.

Although children probably spend more time in school writing true stories from their lives than they spend writing any other genre, they receive very little instruction in that genre. In fact, children tend to write true stories from their lives when they aren't studying the features of a particular genre but are instead focusing on generic topics, such as strategies for revision or writing with details. Many children think they are writing personal narratives when their pieces are not narratives at all but instead are hodge-podges of anything-I-can-think-of-that-relates-to-this-topic pieces about a topic such as "My Trip," "Going to Summer Camp," or "My Baseball Game." Typically in these texts, children accumulate comments, feelings, anecdotes, and information loosely related to a topic. The good news is that when children actually *do* write narratives—and especially Small Moment narratives—their texts tend to be very effective.

PLANNING FOR CHILDREN'S GROWTH IN WRITING

In order to prepare for a unit of study, a teacher must look at what his or her children are already doing as writers and imagine how the unit of study can be multilevel enough to provide each kind of writer with a learning pathway. This was especially important for Abby Oxenhorn and me, because as we entered this unit, many of Abby's kindergarteners were still having problems saying good-bye to their parents and getting to the bathroom. They seemed very, very young to us. In order to plan this unit, we studied what Abby's children were already doing as writers and imagined the way our teaching in conferences and minilessons across this unit could help each of them progress. We found the easiest way to do this was to roughly categorize her children, then to imagine the work we'd do with each particular cluster of writers. Here are several suggestions for how to proceed with writers at different stages.

If children are . . .	You could . . .
A few children may still be drawing nonrepresentational pictures and not writing with letters.	Encourage representational drawings that show the crucial elements of the story. "Where's you in this picture?" "What are you doing?" Then push in ways described below.
Some children might be using accompanying oral language to comment on rather than create a story. That is, when asked, "What will you write?" these children will point to their pictures and create texts that are captions or comments rather than stories. When asked, "What will you write?" such a child might say, "That's me," or "I'm going fast," rather than using story language, such as, "Saturday I went skateboarding. First, I got on the skateboard. It went fast. . . ."	▶ Support storytelling across the day by reading a few favorite stories over and over (books such as Corduroy, Caps for Sale, and fairy tales) and by encouraging children to approximate-read these very familiar, rich stories on their own. All our kindergarteners and many of our first graders study the pictures and tell the accompanying stories. As they know the stories better and internalize more story language and story structure, the stories they tell take on more of the rhythm and language of stories. ▶ Create many opportunities for children to storytell about their lives. "Tell your partner a story that happened to you at recess today." ▶ Elicit and support storytelling in conferences. "Will you tell me the story that goes with your picture? [Silence.] What's happening?" ["That's me skateboarding."] Oh—so does your story go, 'One day I was skateboarding?' [Nod.] Then [turn the page] what did you do next? So you should draw that here! [Turn the page.] Keep going. [Turn the page.] How does it end? Draw that here. So let's go back and remember the whole story. It starts, 'One day I was. . . .' Would you continue it?"
Some children will still be writing strings of letters that seem random (that is, they won't seem to be the result of the child saying a word, segmenting it into phonemes, and then putting the sounds the child hears onto the page).	▶ Notice and support ways their writing-like marks reflect growing knowledge of written language (e.g., top to bottom, left to right, etc.). ▶ Show children how we label drawings: "This is my skateboard, so here I need to write skateboard. Watch how I do it. Skateboard. Skateboard. /sk/-- and then I write S. Now I reread the S and say what I want to write . . ./ska/. Now I will say the word and hear more sounds- /t/- and write t." We reread S as "ska," so that a /t/ sound comes next because we know this particular child will first write with initial and final consonants. After writing st, reread and continue to add on sounds, now saying, "skateboard skateboar /d/ /d/." Write d, and reread as skateboard. "Will you help me label the sun? Say it with me. Sun. Sun. Listen for what you hear first at the start of sun, then write that. [Child does so.] Put your finger under what you just wrote and let's read it: s - /s/. Sun. Sun. What other sounds do you hear? Write that. . . . "

If children are . . .	You could . . .
A few children might try to write fictional stories.	Tell them that for now we are writing small moments of our lives and lure them to find these vignettes equally fascinating.
Some children's stories will seem constrained by a concern for what they can spell.	You can model choosing a moment of time from your life and then enact how you become stymied by spelling, but hurrah, you then get past this. "Let me show you how I write. Let's see . . . I want to tell about how my cousin and I made a fort out of blankets. [Quickly draw and then write my so that you're ready to write cousin.] Wait! Can I spell cousin? Oh no. I don't know how to spell it. I can't write about this [your voice is downcast.] You know what, [your voice is now exultant], I'm going to just do the best I can and keep going!" Later you will come to blankets. "Oh no, I can't write blankets. Maybe I won't tell about the fort. What do you think I should do now?" Elicit the idea that you need to just "do the best you can" until this becomes a mantra.
Most children will write on broad, general topics.	Teach children to focus on specific, small moments. "You've told a lot about your mom. I can see you love her. Can you think of one particular time you had with your mom recently? How did it start? What happened first? You should definitely write that down! So page one will be [such and such], and then what happened? So that'll be page two!"
Some children will write tiny jewels of a story almost by accident.	Be ready to run along behind children, telling them what they just did . . . and making it more likely they will provide an encore.
Some children will write stories that contain only one episode.	Your challenge will be to help children grasp the concept of zooming in on one small moment . . . but to not go overboard with focus. You are hoping they will retell small sequences of events, such as retelling how they built a sand castle, added flags to the towers, then watched the wave wash it away. Be sure the stories you model have a sequence of events. You can always help a child find the small events within a big one (I went to the beach. It was fun).
Some children will write sequential stories, but they may sound more like lists than like stories. (I ride my bike. I ride fast. I ride a lot. I go home.)	These children will benefit from being immersed in a culture of storytelling, from being asked to first tell their stories really well to a partner, and from learning that stories can make listeners worried, excited, scared. . . . Often it's when a writer builds tension in a story that we begin to use language to create drama.

UNDERSTANDING A SMALL MOMENT STORY

GETTING READY

▶ Selected few pages from a familiar, loved text in which a writer has written about small, true moments

▶ Supply of stapled booklets in the writing center, each containing three or four pages—kindergartners may need blank pages, while older children may need space for a picture and a line or two or more for writing

▶ Cleaned-out folder (work from the previous unit should be filed away in the classroom)

◉ See CD-ROM for resources

ONE WAY TO BEGIN THIS UNIT IS TO READ ALOUD *a few pages from a familiar picture book. A carefully chosen excerpt can help children understand what it means for a writer to write about a Small Moment in ways that make that moment seem big. The text you read aloud needs to match what you'll ask your students to do. You will be asking your children to write across a sequence of pages in small booklets. (The pages provide concrete support for the chronological nature of stories.) You'll want your children to learn that in true stories from our lives, one thing happens and then the next and the next.*

This session will use your own writing or a published text to show children that when an author writes a Small Moment story, the author stretches out the sequence of actions across several pages to make the moment feel important and interesting.

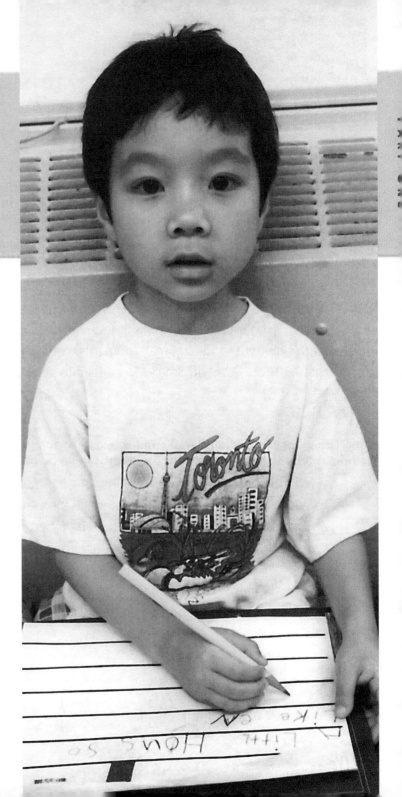

The Minilesson

Connection

Celebrate that your youngsters have been writing true stories from their lives. Tell your students that today they will take Small Moments and stretch them out to make even longer stories.

Abby waited until children had settled in their rug spots and their eyes were on her. "We have been talking a lot over the last few weeks about how writers write about their own lives. As writers, we have been thinking of stories from our own lives, making pictures in our heads and putting our stories on paper. Today we are beginning a new unit of study. Together we're going to learn how writers catch Small Moments from their lives and stretch those moments out, turning Small Moments into stories that cross several pages."

Teaching

Read an excerpt of a familiar exemplar text. Juxtapose the vibrant, detailed story with a limp, bland version in order to highlight the value of details.

Abby held up Vera B. Williams' *A Chair for My Mother*. "I read this aloud to you a few days ago. Today let's notice the way Vera takes a Small Moment and stretches it across a few pages. Remember the part where the mother and her daughter are walking home and they see their building on fire?"

"Vera *could* have told that part quickly in just one or two sentences. Her story *could* have gone like this," Abby spoke blandly and quickly, her intonation suggesting this would have been a very dull story indeed. "'We got home and saw the fire. Everyone was safe.'"

Notice that Abby's teaching is lean. As the year unfurls, our minilessons become longer, but for now, it is very important to keep them tight. We're teaching youngsters that this is a time to listen. It's easiest to do this if we don't ramble!

If you read aloud wonderful literature in order to illustrate a quality of writing that you hope children incorporate in their writing, the problem is that children do not necessarily grasp what qualities of writing make the literature effective.

Abby accentuates the craft-technique she wants her children to notice by showing that the author could have written this content in a different way. This is a very effective way to draw children's attention away from the content only (there was a fire) and toward the author's craftsmanship.

"But *instead* of just telling it like that, Vera decided to *stretch the moment out* by telling us tiny little details. Listen closely."

Continue reading the selected excerpt aloud, pausing briefly to highlight the writing technique you hope children notice—using details to stretch out an important moment.

Abby read slowly, looking intently at the text to show her attention to detail.

> My mother and I were coming home from buying new shoes. I had new sandals. She had new pumps. We were walking to our house from the bus. We were looking at everyone's tulips. She was saying she liked the red tulips and I was saying I liked yellow ones.

"What details!" Abby reread the last bit in admiration, then continued.

> *Then* we came to our block. Right outside our house stood two *big* fire engines. I could see lots of smoke. Tall orange flames came out of the roof.

"I can picture it, can't you?"

> All the neighbors stood in a bunch across the street. Mama grabbed my hand and we ran. My uncle Sandy saw us and ran to us. Mama yelled, "Where's Mother?" I yelled, "Where's my grandma?"

If children intervene with little comments, try—warmly and clearly—to signal that this isn't the time for a big discussion.

Liam was on his knees, his hand waving in the air, "She saw a fire, like the one at the Twin Towers."

Abby spoke warmly, "Yes. There was a fire in this story also. It is so sad, isn't it? But Liam, let's try and think about how Vera gave you such a clear picture of what she saw when there was a fire in her apartment. She stretched out that moment, didn't she?"

Notice the way Abby refers to Vera B. Williams by name often, and even assumes the class can be on a first-name basis with her! It's important that authors live in our classrooms, becoming co-teachers.

Abby is trying to give her children a general image of the sort of thing she hopes they will write. It helps if learners have an image of the whole thing that they are trying to make before striving towards a particular component. It is common, therefore, to begin a unit of study with examples that illustrate the big concept of the unit. You may read aloud a published exemplar, write publicly, or show work by former students.

If you read aloud a portion of a published text in the writing workshop, it will usually be an excerpt of a text the class already knows well. We do this because it is easier for listeners to attend to how a text is written when the text is familiar and because it is easier to appreciate an excerpt if one knows the larger text from which it was taken.

Don't let the particular content of some of children's interruptions lead you to be inconsistent in your message that it is not time for interjections. You can say, "Early on in a minilesson I will talk to you. Your job will be to listen. Then later in the minilesson, I'll ask you to try what I'm teaching, and that's a great time to talk."

Active Engagement

Get your students started thinking about the author's technique: the use of details.

"Writers, will you think in your minds about the tiny details that Vera B Williams added?"

Abby bent her head, touched her forehead and muttered, "They were coming home from buying shoes . . . that's a detail . . . and they passed the . . . uh. . . ."

Stopping midsentence, Abby whispered, "Keep thinking. What else did Vera put in her story that was a little detail?" She was coming home with her mother from buying shoes. They were walking home and they passed. . . ."

Ask students to tell their friends the details they recalled from the text.

Abby waited a few seconds. "Turn and tell a friend the tiny details that Vera B. Williams added to stretch out her Small Moment." The children turned their bodies to face a friend, still sitting cross-legged and knee-to-knee, but now with each child's knees touching the other child's knees.

Signal for the class to come back together and ask them to share the details discussed.

"What were some of the tiny details Vera wrote to stretch out her Small Moment?" Abby rephrased the question, "What did you notice about Vera B. Williams' writing?"

Milo raised his hand. Signaling for him to speak, Abby whispered "Eyes on Milo" to all her children, as if reminding them of something they knew well.

Notice that Abby demonstrates and draws children into the process of recalling the details from the read-aloud text, then she lets them continue doing this without as much reliance on her. This is scaffolding at its best.

Abby uses carefully chosen key phrases often, and in this instance she repeats the phrase "to stretch out her Small Moment" because she wants this to become part of her children's repertoire of writing goals and strategies. Repetition is helpful to all human beings, and especially to young children. Don't try to say the same thing in twenty different ways—settle on one phrase and use it often so that your children internalize it.

You'll need to decide on how you will signal the class to return. You may say, "Writers," and wait. You may start a hum that you teach your children to join in to. You'll be signaling like this many times across every day and so you'll clearly want to plan this ritual and to even have some practice sessions helping children do their parts well.

Asking your children to look at the speaker is one step toward teaching them to listen to each other. You should expect your children's heads to visibly turn when a classmate speaks (teach them that necks allow for heads to turn!). If children visually cue in to the speaker, they are more apt to intellectually cue in as well. Invest a lot of attention in teaching students to listen to each other.

"She wrote one thing and then another and then another," Milo said. "Then she put it together."

"Huh!" Abby's tone suggested Milo had just given her a brand-new and illuminating insight.

To encourage others to take in what Milo has said, Abby repeated his insight as if she was listening to it again, responding to it with wonder. "'She wrote one thing and then another and then another, then she put it together!' You are right. She *did* do that, Milo! That's how Vera slowed her writing down, isn't it?"

"She didn't just say 'We looked for our family,' did she? She said, 'Mama grabbed my hand and we ran. My Uncle Sandy saw us and ran. . . . That's such a helpful observation, Milo."

When one child speaks, be sure the child speaks to the class, not just to you. Your role is to listen as one of the class, drawing the class in to join you in listening. Don't listen-as-teacher, as the solo recipient of what the child says. Regard your role as a model of good listening and notice whether your model is influencing the others to do likewise.

If you wonder why, by some miracle, Abby knows to call on a child who produces such an astute comment, the secret lies in the fact that Abby had overheard many of the children's one-to-one conversations. When she calls on someone, she usually has a good idea what that child will say.

Instead of judging Milo's response, saying, "Good idea," Abby pays Milo the ultimate compliment: She listens to him. By doing so, Abby visibly models listening in such a way that another person's ideas change her own.

Abby rephrases what Milo said, accentuating what Vera Williams did do, and again highlights the technique by reminding children that Vera could have written this differently. Abby adds onto Milo's observation so that what he said becomes all the wiser because Abby has paraphrased it. She does this in a way that suggests she's merely rephrasing Milo's comment. Children are left feeling that this smart observation belongs to Milo.

Sophia raised the hand that wasn't churning the ruffles on her sundress, "Yeah, Vera didn't just say they saw the fire. She told us about the pretty yellow and red flowers they saw."

When children point out particular things the writer has done, remind them that these are techniques toward the writer's larger purpose, which you will explain, was "to stretch out a Small Moment."

"Exactly! Sophia noticed how Vera B. Williams stretched her Small Moment out and made it big. She did this by telling us details like the detail about the yellow and red flowers they saw, right, Sophia?"

Link

Encourage the children to write Small Moments like those written by the author of the exemplar text.

"When you write today, think about taking a Small Moment from your life. Try stretching it out by writing in detail."

Show them the booklets to use.

"We're going to be writing our Small Moments in books so you'll see our writing center has paper like this." Abby opened the pages of the booklet, "When you write your Small Moment, try and stretch it out across these three pages."

.

"Okay, if you are at the red table, go choose your booklets." After the children at the red table had left the writing center, she continued. "Blue table." After a moment, "Green table. Yellow table."

Good writing often shifts between generalization of detail, and this is true of teaching, too. Abby has named the guiding principal, and now she and Sophie collect examples of that guiding principle.

Although teachers try to teach just one idea in a minilesson, we sometimes break this rule. Abby tucks her postscript about paper choice at the end of this minilesson because she knows the sequence of pages in a booklet can provide a valuable scaffold, helping her children think of their stories as one thing that happened, then the next, then the next.

Abby has lots more final comments, but her internal clock is ticking. Teach yourself that less is more. The lean, uncluttered nature of Abby's teaching is a great strength.

TIME TO CONFER

You'll want to organize space and time so children can get started on their writing and so you can move among them, conferring. As Abby's children dispersed, they each collected a booklet from the three trays of paper she'd set out. Each booklet contained three pages, stapled together. Because Abby's children are kindergartners, one tray of booklets had no lines and the booklets in the other trays contained one or two lines for print.

Although you will have told children about writing narratives across the pages in these booklets, chances are good that you will need to show children what is entailed in writing a narrative. Plan on holding lots of conferences in which you scaffold children as they retell a focused vignette from their lives. Study the conferences at right to learn the most essential new conferences for this unit. If some of your writers struggle to tell a coherent story, you may also want to look at the conference "Can You Tell a Story and Show It on the Paper?" Try to see the way all these conferences are similar to each other. This is not a tricky type of conference, and it has tremendous power. Above all, notice that you are shifting children into a storyteller voice and helping them to unroll a focused story across several pages. You want to scaffold a literate, flowing story *even if it is mostly an oral story*, captured through a sequence of pictures and labels.

As you confer today, you'll want to look for a few children who write Small Moment narratives, so that you can celebrate that work in your share session.

This conference in *The Conferring Handbook* may be especially helpful today:

▶ *"Will You Touch Each Page and Say What You'll Write?"*

Also, if you have *Conferring with Primary Writers*, you may want to refer to the following conference:

▶ "Is This a Story about Your Life?"
▶ "Can I Show You How to Write What Happened, First, Then Next, Then Next?"
▶ "Can You Tell a Story and Show It on the Paper?"

Ask a child to read aloud a Small Moment (or read it aloud yourself), reinforcing what you want your writers to notice.

"Writers, listen to Sophie's story. She wrote this." [*Fig. I-1*]

I was at a hotel.
I was in the pool.
Then I went to the hot tub.
Then I saw a hummingbird.
It was red and green.

"I love the way Sophie told us what happened first, next, and last. And I love how she zoomed in and told us details about that hummingbird. *And* I love that she wrote something true that happened in her life. Notice that Sophie labeled her picture. Beside this little bird, she wrote, 'hummingbird' and beside this round pool, she wrote 'hot tub.' Writers do these things. Let's keep trying to write true stories just like Sophie and Vera have done."

It's a lovely touch to put young writers in the same category as published authors and to refer similarly to all these writers as models.

I was at a hotel . . .
Then I went
to the hot tub.
Then I saw a
hummingbird. It was
red and green.

Fig. I-1   Sophie

One session isn't nearly enough to teach children to focus their personal narratives. The upcoming Session II works toward the same objective.

▶ Before or after Session II, you could also repeat this minilesson using a different text, perhaps an excerpt from *Owl Moon* (Yolen) or *The Snowy Day* (Keats). "Yesterday, we looked at the way Vera Williams used details to stretch out her Small Moment. Today let's listen to a Small Moment story that another author wrote, and this time I'd again like you to listen for details."

▶ You could ask the class to contribute to a shared writing story about a Small Moment they experienced together. The class could compose the Small Moment story together in the minilesson, writing either on paper or "in the air" (which means the story could be talked through but not written). You might say, "So if we were going to take lessons from Vera Williams, only instead of writing about seeing our apartment on fire we decide to write about yesterday's field trip to the bakery, we could focus on when we walked in and found all those smells. If we started our story, 'Yesterday we walked to the bakery . . .' would you tell your partner the Small Moment story of our visit to the bakery? 'Yesterday we walked to the bakery. . . .'" You'd then ask the class to turn and talk. Later, you'd elicit one version only. You'd avoid scribing the child's suggestion to prevent the minilesson from becoming a maxilesson.

DISCOVERING ONE SMALL MOMENT

GETTING READY

- Focused vignette from your everyday life; plan how to tell the story of this moment briefly, yet in a way that moves through time (first this happened, then this, and finally this) and includes a detail or two
- Text you used in yesterday's minilesson (perhaps it was *A Chair for My Mother*)
- Little pad and pencil to write what the children say
- Examples of stories that children can judge— Small Moment story or not?
- See CD-ROM for resources

YOU WILL HAVE READ THROUGH YOUR CHILDREN'S WORK *and, in your mind, you'll have a long list of wishes for your kids. You'll wish they'd*

- *Draw more representationally*
- *Write more focused narratives*
- *Write more in addition to drawing*
- *Use their time more wisely*
- *Focus on writing more than on handwriting*

You are wise to wish these things for your writers, but don't show children your feelings if you are discouraged. For now, instead of tackling all the problems, immerse the class in rich examples of what you hope they'll do. Act as if all is going splendidly, even if it isn't yet. Find the good in the classroom even if you know you are overlooking the problems that are really there. Many of the problems will go away with more time. The others, the ones that persist, can be addressed a few days from now when a "We need to fix things that are awry" tone won't deflate the energy in your room.

To follow up on Session I, then, you may decide to demonstrate how you go about writing a Small Moment across the pages in a booklet. Let children in on your thinking by demonstrating how you focus on just a Small Moment and then envision (or remember) that moment so that you can draw and write with detail.

In this session, you will write a story in the air that zooms in on one moment, demonstrating thinking hard and picturing the moment while you put it on the page.

The Minilesson

Connection

Remind the class that they already saw how an author took a Small Moment and turned it into a story. Tell them that today, they can watch *you* do this.

"Yesterday, we saw that Vera Williams decided to write about what happened when she saw her apartment was on fire. We noticed that she didn't tell about the whole day. She told about one little part of the day. She told about walking home from buying shoes, then turning the corner, then seeing the fire truck. Today, I'll show you how I write about Small Moments in my life because all of you will be doing that, too."

Teaching

Write publicly, modeling whatever you want to highlight about the writing process. Show that you *could* have approached this writing with a broad topic in mind, but that, no, you instead zoom in on a more focused topic.

"I *could* write about all the things I did with my dog Tucker yesterday. But no, I am going to zoom in on just how I *gave Tucker a bath!* Writers do that. We zoom in on just a small part."

Model how writers envision their stories in their minds and sketch the stories, bit by bit, across pages.

"So I'm remembering giving Tucker a shampoo."

I am demonstrating by writing publicly. It is almost as if I take the top off my head and let children see the wheels in my brain turn. But, of course, the strategies I spotlight for kids aren't necessarily those that I actually use as I (as an adult) write. Instead I demonstrate and highlight strategies I see as within grasp of the kids.

Here I use a phrase over and over that I hope will become part of the writing vocabulary in the classroom. Writers "zoom in on Small Moments." I find it helps to make a funneling motion with my hands in to help children understand the term "zooming in."

Be sure your selected moment is an ordinary one to which children can relate. Perhaps when it was time to go to school you couldn't find your shoe, looked all over, and found it in a weird place. Perhaps you were making cookies and didn't have an ingredient so you substituted something different instead—and it turned out okay, or awful. You'll probably want your story to contain a problem that gets resolved (although don't say this to kids). It's great if even these very small stories have some emotional content. Children will respond to a story in

"Oh! I can picture how it went like a movie in my head. What came first?" I put my hand on my head to dramatize that I took time to envision the event.

"Oh, yeah, I dragged Tucker over to the tub. She shrank back." I acted out how Tucker shrank back.

"I am going to sketch that on the page so that I remember what happened first in my story." I sketched quickly.

Turning to the next blank page, I said, "I lifted Tucker into the tub and said, 'Don't be scared.'" I sketched this on page two. Then I slowly turned the page to build anticipation of what came next in the story. "Next I'm going to say, 'Soon she had soap bubbles all over her head!'"

Active Engagement

Ask students to tell their friend what they noticed that you did as a writer.

"Turn and tell your friend what you noticed me doing as a writer when I wrote my Small Moment. Children shifted their bodies and for two minutes discussed what they saw the teacher do.

William: "Lucy thought of a story in her life."

Lily: "She pictured it in her head."

William: "Yeah, yeah and then she drew it down on her paper."

Help the class generate a short list of observations. Write down what the students say in a chart that will become a reference.

"Will someone share what you discussed with your friend? What did I do when I wrote my Small Moment?" Soon I had written this chart.

which you said good-bye to your friend, walked sadly away from her house, and then sat on a stoop to write her a letter.

I try to act out the idea that my head functions almost like a movie projector, showing a movie that when I remember an incident it is almost as if I replay the movie of that incident in my mind. This is a complicated but important image. I'm trying to make it more likely that children retell their small moments rather than summarizing or talking about them.

You need not actually write the story—and doing so slows down the minilesson. It's okay to "write in the air."

Notice that my persona has just switched. For a time, I was almost role-playing being a writer, composing in front of children. Now I've resumed my teacher identity and am talking about writing and their work. You'll see teachers shift in and out of the role of being a writer (this is when we actually feel like actors).

WRITING SMALL MOMENTS

Writers think of something that happened to them.

They picture it in their minds.

They sketch it on the paper.

They write words.

This chart will vary based on your children's responses.

Notice the chart is labeled "Writing Small Moments." That is the name Abby and I give, within her classroom, to the kind of writing her children are doing. Abby and I don't often use the term "personal narrative writing" because these are kindergartners, and we love the phrase "Small Moment stories." Another teacher may want to use other synonyms, calling this unit "true stories" or "personal narrative."

Link

Review the list by telling students they will do all these things when they write their own stories today and every day.

"Today and every day, you'll be doing all these things. Before you go from the rug, think about the story you began yesterday. Close your eyes and remember the moment you are writing about." I paused and did this, signaling for them to do so as well. "Thumbs up if you are remembering that one time. Can you picture in your mind what happened first . . . and then next? Thumbs up if you can. Okay, Sofie, you can get started writing your story. Jason, Krishna, off you go. Remember to make a movie in your mind, then draw and write. Okay, Evan. . . ."

It is more powerful than you realize to demonstrate pausing and thinking. You needn't articulate your thoughts. Simply taking time to recall, and doing this in front of kids, makes an impression.

MID-WORKSHOP TEACHING POINT

Stop the class to celebrate that one student decided to stay with his piece, adding more to it, stretching it out.

"Class, may I stop you? I have to tell you about a great thing I saw Sergio do today. When I was conferring with him, he was about to stop the book he was working on about a basketball game and start a new book. But then Sergio reread his piece and decided to *stay with* his basketball story. He decided to say more about what happened during his basketball game. He didn't have room in his booklet, so I showed him how to tape on lines so that he could keep stretching out his Small Moment. It's an incredible thing that Sergio, who is only five years old, is doing just like real writers do, adding more paper to say more about his story! Sergio, I am so happy you decided to stay with your piece and not just jump into a new story. Children, if any of you want to stay with a book for longer like Sergio has done and you need lines, just ask me or Angel's mom and we will help you."

You are lucky indeed if you can recruit some of your children's parents to help in a writing workshop.

When I make such a fuss about the amazing thing Sergio has done, it's totally clear that others will do likewise. Sergio taped a small strip of paper containing a few blank lines onto his paper, then filled the lines up with print. I suggest that Angel's mom can help children tape similar flaps onto their papers.

TIME TO CONFER

Each day, as your writers work, they draw on a growing repertoire of what you have taught them to do. By now, they will have learned to choose topics that are narratives; to plan their stories in their minds and, as they turn the pages of a booklet, to draw and then add even more detail; to say what they'll write and then locate the first word from the sentence; to say that word slowly, isolating and recording the first sound; and more. All of this is at their disposal, and you hope they draw on each strategy as needed.

The truth is your task is similar. You also have a growing repertoire of what you can do, and you, also, need to draw on whatever seems appropriate from that repertoire. If you ever feel empty-handed as a teacher of writing, recall earlier minilessons or earlier conferences, and remember today's work should incorporate all you've learned on previous days. Keep in mind that old lessons need to be relearned over and over. The writers in your care will seem able to do something, but then when they move on to tackle more complex tasks, they will probably no longer be able to do what once seemed easy. For example, children at this level still need to be able to finish one piece and start another without teacher intervention. They still need to go back to finished work and add details. They still need to be willing to approximate, to say, "I'll do the best I can and keep going." Meanwhile, however, try one also focusing on writing sequential narratives.

These conferences in *The Conferring Handbook* may be especially helpful today:

▶ *"Will You Touch Each Page and Say What You'll Write?"*

▶ *"Let Me Help You Put Some Words Down"*

▶ *"As a Reader, I'd Love to Hear More About That"*

Also, if you have *Conferring with Primary Writers*, you may want to refer to the conferences in part two.

After-the-Workshop Share

Call children together on the carpet. Tell them that a lot of children have asked you, "Is _this_ a Small Moment?"

"Today a lot of you have come up to me and showed me your story, asking, 'Is this okay?' I think you meant, 'Is this a _Small Moment?_' Today I want to teach you how _you_ can be a writing teacher _for each other!_ When Sam brings me his story and says, 'Is this a Small Moment?' I listen and ask myself: Is it a _true_ story? Is it about a _Small Moment?_ Does it make sense?"

Ask students to judge if a story is a Small Moment by listening to examples.

"Can you _all_ be writing teachers with me today? Let's listen to Sam's story and then let's ask ourselves those three questions. Listen to Sam's story."

I went to the museum. We saw big, big dinosaurs. I touched one with my hand. Then I went home.

"So if Sam asked you, 'What do you think? Is this a Small Moment story?' What could you say? Does it do these three things?"

James: "It is true and when he touched it, it is a Small Moment."

Tiffany: "But it's a different time, when he went home. Maybe you could leave that out."

"I loved that detail about the touch too. Now let's listen to Nicholas's story and again, you will be a writing teachers. Ask yourself, 'Is it a true story? Is it about a Small Moment? Does it make sense?'" [_Fig. II-1_]

"Tell your friend whether this is a true story about a Small Moment. Does it make sense?"

The children turned to talk, and most agreed that yes, Nicholas' story fit the bill as a Small Moment story.

Fig. II-1   Nicholas

The Hug That Hurt
After children's center I went to Jonathan's house because my parents were at work.

Jonathan gave me a big hug that hurt a little in the middle.

Then I said, "Jonathan, that's enough." Then I said, "Jonathan, that's enough again." The end.

As often as you can, involve children in assessing their own narratives. This is a powerful way to teach children to apply criteria.

- Repeat the same minilesson using another vignette from your life. We offered suggestions for finding Small Moment stories from your own life during the teaching component of this minilesson.

- Tell children the story of one time when you were going to write a Small Moment. Angle the story of your writing in a way that shows your children that you had to learn whatever it is you want them to learn. For example, perhaps your children seem to value only grand topics such as birthdays, sleepovers, or big trips, and you want to show that everyday life is worth writing about. Retell your own writing life to show how you got past this problem. "Let me show you what happened when I was learning to write Small Moment stories," you might say. "I thought, 'Hmm. What would be a great story?' And, I remembered long, long, long, ago when I went on an airplane trip to Disneyland. But my writing teacher said to me, 'Lucy, don't write about a Huge Trip that happened long ago. Write about a little moment that happened today, or yesterday.' And I said, 'Not much happened.' And he said, 'A million Small Moments happened.' And you know what—he was right. We made a list. I woke up and the sun was shining so I put my pillow over my head. (That's one moment, one story.) I made a pile of pancakes for breakfast, but my dog climbed up in my chair and ate them! (That's another moment, another story.)"

- You may want to slow down and make more of the concept of zooming in. Make or show a wide-angle picture and contrast it with a zoomed-in one of the same scene. You could use Istvan Banyai's picture book, *Zoom*, to make your point.

Productivity

Take your children's folders home and look through the work they've accomplished in this new unit. Look with a range of different lenses.

One lens you'll want to use is the lens of productivity. How much work has each child produced since the unit began, and what do you make of this? When you look through each and every child's work you'll see work that hasn't had the benefit of one-to-one instruction. "How could she have accomplished so little?" you'll ask yourself. Sometimes you won't find any rationale for her disappointing work. You will wrack your brains, trying to remember the child's behavior during writing time.

The truth is, sometimes children have started, abandoned, and discarded work. Those pieces may be in the trash, and this is why it looks as if they've done nothing. Other times children have been socializing so much during writing time that they haven't gotten a lot of writing done. Then, too, sometimes the intricacies of the illustrations have lured children away from writing. You'll want to address these issues.

Sequential Narratives

Another lens you'll want to use is that of sequence. Can your able children write sequential narratives?

▸ Some children regard their sentences as captions not stories. On page after page, these children might write, "Here I am . . ." or "This is my mom. . . ." You'll want to intervene and get these children telling and then writing stories.

▸ Some children (like Henry [*Fig. II-2*]) will have written all-about subjects, listing their attributes rather than retelling what happened one time. Gather a small group of children who do this and point out that a writer could write all about the meeting area (listing descriptors) or the writer could tell what happened first, next, and next in a meeting area.

You'll want to use other lenses as well to look at childrens' work. How are children doing with high frequency words? With word endings? With writing in lowercase letters? With punctuation? With endings to their stories? Examining student work through any of these lenses can prove helpful. If I study this particular story by Danielle, for example, these are the things I notice.

▸ I can read her writing and so can she. [*Fig. II-3*]

▸ Danielle for the most part represents the major sounds in a word with a letter that is well chosen (if not correct). For example, she spells *tired* as *tiyrd*.

▸ She fills up the space given to her (suggesting to me that steering her toward paper that contains another two lines for print would be great).

▸ She doesn't rely on sight words much.

▸ She is a fearless writer, generating content with no worry for the spelling consequences.

Fig. II-2   Henry

Fig. II-3   Danielle

- Danielle comes close to writing an All-About piece listing the attributes of one event rather than writing a sequential narrative. Encouraging her to write the story of what she did (using the pronoun 'I' not 'we') would help.
- Her stories are underdeveloped and could profit from more detail.

My hunch is that Danielle is ready to move into conventional reading, if she isn't already doing it, and that her writing will zoom forward as she spends more time immersed in print and in written conventions.

ESTABLISHING LONG-TERM PARTNERSHIPS

GETTING READY

- Student (or better yet, an adult) ready to act as your writing partner
- List of partnerships you've planned
- Stack of papers, each with two names to represent a partnership, arranged around the meeting area as a partnership seating chart
- Paper with your name and your partner's name with which to demonstrate
- See CD-ROM for resources

YOU HAVE GIVEN CHILDREN TIME EACH DAY TO WRITE, *tools they need, models of what others have written, and instruction. All this is necessary— but not sufficient. Writers also need company.*

You will have given children chances to talk during "turn-and-talk" interludes in your minilessons. These tiny conversations will happen more efficiently and be more valuable if each child returns to the same partner each day.

Some teachers suggest that partners sit beside each other during minilessons and shares and also write near each other. This doesn't mean they coauthor texts; they don't. It does mean that when a teacher offers some mid-workshop advice, the teacher can say, "Would you reread your work to your partner?" or "Would partners check to see if both of you have put words onto your pages? If you haven't done this, help each other and do it now," and these conversations can involve a minimum of fuss.

Sometimes, while listening to partner conversations, it seems as if their only value is that writers get "air time" in which they can expound on their topics. As any writer will agree, this alone can be valuable.

This minilesson will establish partnerships and also will give partners jobs to do together. For today, partners will revisit what each child did the preceding day, and they'll plan for upcoming work. These are tall orders, so don't be surprised if some of your children hear only half of your directions.

THE MINILESSON

Connection

Convene your class, steering them to new seats. Tell your children that they have most of the conditions writers need to write.

"Writers, as you come to the meeting area today, I need each of you to find the paper that has your name on it and to sit where your name is."

"Writers, we've talked a lot about what writers need to do their best work. We know writers need tools," I held up markers, pens, folders, and date stamps to illustrate, "and you have your toolboxes. We know writers need paper, so you have your booklets." I held up paper.

Add one more thing: Writers need company. Show children how to plan with a partner.

"Today I want to tell you one more *huge* thing writers need. Sometimes, to get our thinking going, writers talk with other writers. We need company. We need a writing friend, or two. And often, we get together with one person who becomes our special writing friend—our writing partner—and plan what we will write."

Tell children that today they'll plan with a writing partner.

"You'll see your name and your partner's name on a piece of paper. You'll see that the papers say that one of you is partner one and one is partner two. Every day, for every minilesson and every share from now on, you and your partner will sit at the place where your names are now, beside each other. And I've changed your seats during writing time so you'll sit near your writing partner during writing time too. Later when you go off to write, you can find your new writing seats."

My minilesson today is different than the others. Until now, minilessons in this unit have moved children toward writing focused, sequential narratives. This minilesson instead establishes a structure that will last across the year. I also occasionally interrupt the flow of teaching about writing to address management issues.

Writing, like teaching, can be a lonely enterprise because there are ways in which both are always done alone. How crucial it is that the solitude of writing (like the solitude of teaching) is balanced and supported by intervals of collaboration.

This is just one possible way to manage the chaos this minilesson threatens to create. Often teachers will find other solutions. The real point is that we need to predict when our teaching ideas will have management ramifications, and to find ways to maintain efficiency and order.

"So far, we've been planning by thinking in our own minds about our stories. But writers also plan by talking with a writing friend, or partner. Today we're going to use writing partners to help us plan."

Teaching

Demonstrate how writers share previously written work and discuss future writing.

"Let me show you how writers plan with their partners. Watch closely because this is what you are going to be doing from now on. Abby will be my partner. First, notice we already have a bit of floor space where we will meet today and every day. This is our partner place." Abby and I had our names written large on a piece of paper that was exactly like the papers containing other partnership names.

"Next we will decide who goes first. Partner one will and that's me. So I read my story to Abby." I did. "Now, I'll tell my partner what I will write today—and part of that means we'll talk about if I'm done with yesterday's story or if I'm going to continue working on it. And I'll tell my partner what I might say in today's story. Watch." Abby and I did this talking.

"Now I am going to ask Abby, 'What are *you* going to write today?'"

"I'll write about getting a dog," said Abby.

"'How will your story go?' I'm really going to listen to her answer."

Abby answered by telling the words of the story she'd soon write.

"So now we both have plans for writing and we can get started!"

Have two children demonstrate what writing partners do for each other.

"Let's watch as one of our partnerships gets started. Okay, Jan and Greg. You are partners. We are going to admire how you get started." They turned and sat, facing each other. "Oh great, they are sitting knee to knee. Greg, ask Jan, 'What did you write yesterday?'" He did.

In response, Jan got her booklet out and read it to Greg. "Don't you love the way Jan is reading her story to her partner? I wonder if Greg will ask her, 'Are you done or will you add on to that story today?'" Greg does this and soon he was listening to the new bits Jan planned to add.

Prior to this minilesson, you need to mentally divide the class into partnerships. Consider ability levels, friendships, and behavior issues. These partnerships will probably be mixed-ability partnerships (although certainly don't set one partner up as the teacher for the other). If you need to have a threesome, be careful because this can be a difficult social arrangement.

Partnerships are especially important if some of your students are English language learners because these children need language input more than anything. Try to partner children so that no two who speak Mandarin are partners. If you aren't certain which child speaks which language, you need to find out. Ask the class for help. You'll also find it helpful to partner children so that one has stronger English skills than the other. Under no circumstances can you allow an English language learner to be isolated because "he doesn't speak English." The child needs just the opposite!

Surprise, surprise! Greg follows my suggestion to the T!

Active Engagement

Ask children to begin their partnerships in the way they've just seen.

"Will each of you turn to your partner now? Partner two, will you ask your partner the same questions? Ask, 'What did you write yesterday?' And then, like Greg, ask, 'Are you done or will you add on today?' Get started."

Link

Tell them they will write alone, and then they'll join their partners.

"Writers, all your life you are going to want to have conversations like this one in which you share and plan writing. For now, we'll work alone, but in about twenty minutes, you'll regroup with your partner."

MID-WORKSHOP TEACHING POINT

Ask children to share their writing by having one partner read to the other and then talk about the writing. The two writers can take turns.

"Writers, may I interrupt? It has been great for me to hear your stories today. Your partners are probably dying to hear what you've written too. So put partner two's story between the two of you, as if this were reading time and you were about to read a book together. Thumbs up when you've done this. Okay. Now, will partner two read your writing to partner one? Partner two, point at the words. If you have trouble, help each other. And when you finish, have a talk like we had this morning. Ask, 'Will you add on or are you done?' and get the writer to say the exact words he or she will write. After you've both read to each other and talked with each other, get back to work."

Don't hesitate to put words into your children's mouths. These questions can launch children into a lifetime of good conversations. Many children profit from explicit instruction even in something like having conversations with each other. If children don't know that in conversations, the conversation should keep going back and forth between two people, then tell them this explicitly.

Notice that in my minilesson, I am explicit not just when I initiate an activity but also when I teach writers that the strategy we have worked on is one they'll use for their whole lives.

The words we select matter. Woven into my instructions are lots of assumptions. I assume children are dying to share, for example. We teach a lot by what we assume.

Time to Confer

Because this minilesson supports children planning their stories out in the company of a long-term partner, you may want to involve partners in your conferring. That is, if you talk with one writer, you may want the writer's partner to be alongside you as you confer.

If the writer's story is a little confusing, you might say this to the partner. "I'm a little confused about what happened, aren't you? Let's ask the writer to tell the story again and see if we can figure out what happened first," I touch one finger, "then next," I touch the next finger, "and next." I touch the next finger. "So watch how I tell the writer that I'm a little confused." The conferences at the right should provide an important template for you.

If the writer's partner and I both understand the story best if it is mostly an oral story, not a written one, I again will rope the partner in on the job of helping the writer record more of the text. "Aren't you wondering why she didn't write any of this great story?" I'll say to the partner. "We better ask. Watch how I do that. . . ." See "Let Me Help You Put Some Words Down" from *The Conferring Handbook*.

These conferences in *The Conferring Handbook* may be especially helpful today:

▸ *"Will You Touch Each Page and Say What You'll Write?"*
▸ *"Let Me Help You Put Some Words Down"*
▸ *"As a Reader, I'd Love to Hear More About That"*

Also, if you have *Conferring with Primary Writers*, you may want to refer to the following conferences:

▸ "Can I Show You How to Write What Happened, First, Then Next, Then Next?"
▸ "Can You Tell a Story and Show It on the Paper?"

After-the-Workshop Share

After you gather the children, let them practice talking *quietly* with each other about their writing and then turning to you.

"I know you can't wait to hear what your partner wrote! This time, let's practice talking to our partner in one-inch voices. So when I say, 'Tell your partner what you wrote about,' you will whisper your topic to your partner, talking in a one-inch voice. Then, when I say, 'Look at me,' I would like everyone to stop talking instantly and look up at me. Let's try that. Tell your partner what you wrote about." I gave them two minutes. Nicole "read" her story. [*Fig. III-1*] "Look at me. Good job. You may talk again with your partners. Tell each other what you'll do next." After two minutes, I said, "Look at me." I paused for their eyes to find me. "Let's keep this tone in mind tomorrow when we plan with our partners."

Children need explicit instructions about how to manage the transitions in a school day. Children need to know how to move from listening to you in a minilesson or a share to talking softly to each other, then back to listening carefully to you. They will make these transitions often throughout the day.

I was in the elevator with my mom.
I pushed the button. I fell down. I was sad.
My mom said, "You'll be okay."

Fig. III-1 Nicole

IF CHILDREN NEED MORE TIME

Reinforce the partnerships you've established today by using them often. The share session can be a time to support the partnerships. You won't want to do another minilesson right away on partnerships because you will need to maintain the momentum of your Small Moments unit. But you can continue to teach in ways that lift the work occurring in partnerships up a notch. Your instruction will just have to be woven into your share sessions, small group strategy lessons or into your time of giving mid-workshop advice. When children do meet with their partners, it's best to keep your instructions the same for now. Ask writers to share what they've written and to tell each other the exact words they will write next.

▸ You may notice that instead of actually sharing their work, many children will just tilt their pages towards their partners. You can show them that it isn't enough to talk about writing; show them that partners put one story between them. The writer reads the text, probably pointing under the print. If the writer has trouble, the writer rereads, recalls what he or she wants to say, relies on the picture, and so on. If the writer finds words were deleted, he or she can fix things up.

▸ Then, too, children are apt to tell partners the topics they plan to address in the day ahead instead of actually saying the words they intend to write. If one child says, "I'm going to write about my dog," you'll want to encourage that child's partner to nudge for the actual text by asking, "How will your story go?"

STRETCHING ONE SMALL MOMENT

GETTING READY

▶ An exemplar text (perhaps Audrey Penn's *The Kissing Hand*, although Jane Chelsea Aragon's *Salt Hands* is equally magical)
▶ Chart paper and marker
⊙ See CD-ROM for resources

THIS UNIT BEGAN WITH CHILDREN LISTENING to a *Small Moment* contained within Vera Williams' book, *A Chair for My Mother*. In this session, children will listen to another published author's *Small Moment*. This time their perspective will be a bit different; they'll listen as insiders because they have tried their hands at Small Moment writing.

It is important to marinate youngsters in stories like those we hope they will write. *The Kissing Hand* is one such story; you'll want to read it as a read-aloud book without commentary before and after this minilesson. It is a fictional story about a family of raccoons, not a personal narrative, but children will overlook that characters are raccoons and identify instantly with this sweet story of family love.

In today's lesson, you'll say, "Listen to this story—it's rather like those you all are writing." This may sound like a simple lesson, but imagine if a teacher said to you, "Listen to this book—it reminds me of the writing you did yesterday." How your heart would soar! And you'd write better because of this association.

After you invite children to listen to how a published author stretches a moment across several pages, you'll ask children to research your writing process. Model how you go about writing a similar story of your own. In your demonstration, you'll touch each page and plan the words you'll write on that page.

This lesson encourages children to learn from other authors who tell Small Moment stories across the pages of their books. You'll encourage your children to plan their own writing in the presence of partners by touching each page and saying what they will write on that page.

Connection

Celebrate the fact that children are writing their Small Moments in booklets and that the stories go across several pages. Tell them that today you'll study an author who does this too.

"Writers, I took your stories home last night and read them, and I realized you guys have learned so much! You used to just write one page and you'd cram the whole story on one page like, 'I was skateboarding and then I fell but I am okay and I had fun.'"

"Now you write in booklets and you stretch your story out over pages like real authors do. The pages help you become like real authors; you put one thing that happened, then you turn the page. Then the next thing happened, then you turn the page. Then you put how it all turned out at the end." Abby acted this out as she spoke. "So I'm glad you are writing in booklets and that you are writing like real authors. Earlier we saw how Vera B. Williams stretched her story of the fire across pages. She said, 'My mother and I were coming home from buying new shoes. . . . We were looking at everyone's tulips,'" Abby turned an imaginary page. "Then we came to our block, and so on."

"Today, let's look closely at another author who writes a lot like you. Listen to how Audrey Penn stretched out a Small Moment in *The Kissing Hand*, making that moment cross several pages just like you do in your writing."

Teaching

Tell children that you will read an excerpt from a book and ask children to notice how the author takes a Small Moment and stretches it out.

Abby leaned forward, "You know the story of *The Kissing Hand*. This time when I read part of it to you, listen for and think about how Audrey Penn *streeeetched* this moment out across several pages." Abby pulled her hands apart to emphasize the idea of stretching something out.

Abby's voice conveys that the old way of writing resulted in stories that were crammed and that in contrast, the new way of writing allows stories to be more expansive.

As you describe the way children stretch their stories out across the pages of their booklets, gesture to show how the turn of the page reinforces the progress in the children's stories.

In earlier minilessons, we've seen that one way to highlight a way of writing is to show two contrasting examples, one that does and one that doesn't illustrate that way of writing. Here we see a second, very effective way to highlight a particular technique. Notice that Abby gives several examples all in a row, and for each example she shows only the salient feature. She shows how the children tell stories that go across pages, how Vera Williams did the same, and then sets them up to hear how Audrey Penn follows suit! Meanwhile the unspoken message is, "You guys are just like these remarkable authors whom we adore."

Krishna interrupted, "You look like you are stretching out gum with your hands like that but you mean to stretch out a story. Right?"

"Krishna—it *is* kind of like gum. You are taking something small and stretching it long. You take a Small Moment and make it go across a lot of pages, telling it long! Okay, listen closely and watch as I turn the pages."

Remind children of how the excerpt fits into the larger story, and then read the Small Moment excerpt aloud, voicing the turn of the page.

"Now remember the part when Chester was leaving for school for the first time and he decided to give his mom the Kissing Hand. That is the Small Moment I will read."

> That night, Chester stood in front of his school and looked thoughtful. Suddenly, he turned to his mother and grinned. "Give me your hand," he told her.

Abby whispered, "Turn the page," and she turned to the next page.

> Chester took his mother's hand in his own and unfolded her large, familiar fingers into a fan. Next, he leaned forward and kissed the center of her hand.

"Turn the page."

> "Now you have a Kissing Hand, too," he told her. And with a gentle "Good-bye" and "I love you," Chester turned and danced away.

Abby stopped for a minute to let her children absorb the story. "Audrey Penn took a tiny moment when Chester gave his mom the Kissing Hand, and Audrey told her moment bit-by-bit, page-by-page, like you guys do."

Active Engagement

Ask the children to research the way you take a Small Moment and stretch it across pages.

"I am going to take a booklet and tell my story of getting the flu shot at the doctor to my partner. Felecia, will you be my partner? I am going to stretch the story out across the pages like Audrey does. Be researchers; watch and listen closely."

The image of stretching something out will resurface at several points across the year. Children will also learn to stretch a word out, listening for, and recording sounds. Eventually they'll think about stretching a metaphor out across pages of a booklet.

Abby chooses an excerpt that is close to the length of what her kindergartners can write. Notice that before she reads this excerpt, she contextualizes it, showing how the excerpt fits into the larger story.

Sometimes I teach older students that stories often begin with the main character doing something or saying something. It is interesting to notice how often stories start in one of those two ways.

By this time in the year, Abby doesn't need to explicitly point out that when she says, "Be researchers," that means her children will soon turn and tell their partners what they saw their teacher doing.

Demonstrate how to write about a Small Moment across several pages.

Abby then held the booklet out beside Felecia and touched the first page, saying, "I am going to write this: 'At the doctor's office I sat on the metal table. The doctor told me to put out my arm.'" Then, after dramatically pausing for a moment to be sure all eyes were on her, Abby whispered, "Turn the page."

Now she touched the second page and said aloud what she would write on that page, "'I turned my head away and closed my eyes so I wouldn't see them give me the shot. I felt a tiny prick.'" Again, Abby paused to be sure all eyes were on her as she turned to the next blank page.

Abby touched the third and final page and said, "'I felt the Band-Aid go on my arm. "You're done," the doctor said. I opened my eyes and realized he was smiling. I smiled back.'"

Ask children to tell their partners what they saw her do.

"Think in your mind for a minute what you saw me do." Abby closed her eyes, touching her temple in a way that clued the children in that they were to do likewise. Many of the children closed their eyes as if they were thinking really hard.

"Who can tell me what I did?"

Sofie said, "You touched each page and told your partner that part of your story." Abby repeated Sofie's words back to the class. "Exactly, I touched each page and told my partner that part of my story."

Link

Send some children off with a reminder to plan their story, touching each page as they do.

"If you are going to start a new book today, before you do, would you get a blank book and practice stretching out your story by touching each page and saying aloud your story, just like I did? Then say to your partner, 'Can I show you how my book might go?' and again, touch each page and say what you'll write on that page. You are writing Small Moments like Audrey Penn's Small Moment and mine. Let's watch the red table as they get started doing this."

Five children stood and headed back to their tables where they had already laid out their work. Two stopped at the writing center for new booklets. The others sat down to work on their ongoing pieces.

Notice that Abby's story begins with the main character—Abby—doing or saying something very particular.

Abby's minilesson today is more full than usual—there will be times when we decide to come on stronger in our minilessons, and Abby is doing so in this instance.

The important thing is to plan your minilessons by focusing on what you want the children to be doing physically, yes, but mostly mentally. How will you recruit their minds, their attention? If you want children to listen to you carefully, you'll profit from saying so. "Listen, because in a minute I will ask you. . . ." If you want children to think about how they'll draw their story, first give them time to recall their stories. Model that you are taking a quiet moment to recall your story, but don't speak during such a moment or your topic will fill their minds. Then quietly steer them to think about whatever you want them to do next. Again, let your own mind do what you want their minds doing. In this instance, Abby asks her children to "Think in your mind for a minute about what it was that you just saw me do." Then, sitting in front of the class, Abby does this herself. Beautiful teaching!

As you send some children off, help those remaining on the rug notice the good work their classmates are doing as they get started.

"Oh, look! George has a brand new empty booklet, let's watch and see if he thinks up his story and then touches each page as he says it aloud," Abby speaks loudly enough that George, of course, follows instructions perfectly, as do all the other children. "Look, he's doing it! Let's watch the green table, then, and see if they do this too. . . ."

Use this technique often to make it likely that children let the minilesson steer their actions during the workshop.

MID-WORKSHOP TEACHING POINT

Remind children to follow their own advice from the chart they complied about what writers do.

"Writers, may I stop all of you? I want to remind you that writers do these things."

> ### WRITING SMALL MOMENTS
>
> Writers think of something that happened to them.
>
> They picture it in their minds.
>
> They sketch it on the paper.
>
> They write words.

As she read the chart aloud, Abby asked students to raise their thumbs if they'd done it, or point to the place in their writing where the work was.

"If any of you haven't done all these things, be sure you do! I notice that some of you haven't written your words yet—you better get going on that."

Most of the charts that you create with the children are meant to function as reference tools. Usually, if a chart isn't useful enough to use constantly, it isn't worth making. You'll need to teach children to refer back to these charts again and again in the middle of their work. You may want to put icons next to the items on the chart to help the children who can't read the words understand them.

TIME TO CONFER

Books on the teaching of writing emphasize that conferences can't be planned; instead we look closely at what children do and respond to what we see. But there are patterns to our conferences, and one pattern is this: Early in a unit of study, we tend to confer to create excitement in the room over the new work. On days one, two, and three in a new unit of study, we try to be sure that lots of writers get the gist of whatever we are trying to establish in the class. Conferences that support the main direction of the minilesson and to allow us to find (and create) good exemplars among the children's work. We then read these aloud. In this way, we use the kids who are well launched in the unit to bring the others along. Within a few days, we will confer especially with children who need a boost.

Today, you may want to use your conferences to ensure that children are applying the advice of the minilesson. If so, tell children you're going to admire the way they do what you've just taught.

Abby and I often begin the workshop by watching, and today we noticed that some of her English language learners strung together their sentences with "ands" only, so we taught them some transition words to use: "one day," "after that," "finally." Several children needed help stretching words out and recording sounds. We reminded another to include details in her pictures and stories. Your children may require something very different, as in the conference reminding Ethan to sketch, not draw.

These conferences in *The Conferring Handbook* may be especially helpful today:

- *"Will You Touch Each Page and Say What You'll Write?"*
- *"Let Me Help You Put Some Words Down"*
- *"As a Reader, I'd Love to Hear More About That"*

Also, if you have *Conferring with Primary Writers*, you may want to refer to the following conference:

- "Writers Make Time to Write Words"

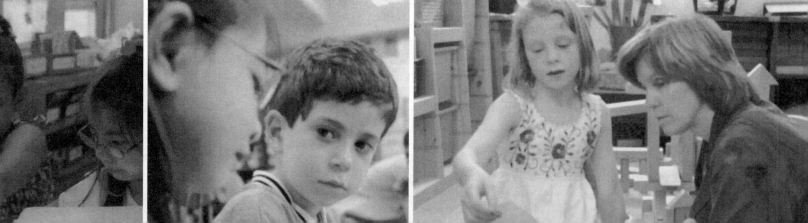

After-the-Workshop Share

Call the children to the carpet. Have a child explain that when she stretched her story out on paper, it was more detailed and sequenced.

"Writers, I want to show you a great example of zooming in and of writing a about tiny moment. Clarissa could have written about her whole day, but she zoomed in on just that moment before school when she's watching TV and her dad says, 'Get ready' and turns off the TV. Listen to her story." [*Fig. IV-1*]

"What Clarissa did is what writers do all the time. She zoomed in on one tiny part of one day and wrote about it with details. Great work! I know many of you, like Clarissa, are zooming in on a tiny, tiny moment."

Examples of great zoomed-in writing may not be examples of great writing but are worthy of holding up nonetheless. This is true for all of our examples—a child who stretches out a word very well may not choose the correct letters to write, but the job may well still be well done and worthy of attention.

The first day of school
The same thing every day.

THE FRS DAY OF SCHOOL
THE S M TAJNO AYT DAH

This is this morning when I was watching TV. I wasn't paying attention to my dad.

TAS IS THE SMOWS
WN I WS WOCING TV
I WAST PAKING ATNTOMYDAD

Then he turned the TV off. Then I got ready.

TN HY TRO THE TV OOF
TN i GT GRTs

Fig. IV-1   Clarissa

Tell your children that students in older grades are also trying to write true narratives, and read a story that could be an important model for your class.

"Did you know that Mrs. Bleichman's first graders are writing Small Moments just like you guys? I visited yesterday and talked with Sudhir. He decided to write about how he got a belt in tae kwan do but instead of telling *all about* the whole thing, he zoomed in on just the moment he woke up, like Clarissa did. Listen." [*Fig. IV-2*]

Notice the difference and similarities between the kindergarten and the first-grade text. The two texts were representative of what most children were doing in early October in Abby Oxenhorn's kindergarten and in Pat Bleichman's first grade. Pat Bleichman is the coauthor of our unit of study on revision.

It was Thursday morning. Suddenly I woke up. "It's my belt test!" I shouted very loudly as I jumped on my bed. Then my mom came into my room. She asked me what's so exciting? "My belt test! My belt test!"

I was so proud of myself. I was going to get my high yellow belt in Tae Kwon Do!

Fig. IV-2   Sudhir

▸ Repeat this lesson but focus more specifically on the planning that writers do. Perhaps show your children that you say the pages over in your mind until it sounds like a story and until the three pages go together in a story-like way. Demonstrate touching each page and saying what you will write as you stretch out your story. As the active engagement, you could give each child a blank booklet and have him or her try rehearsing for writing this way.

▸ Compare two pieces that you or a child wrote where one is an undeveloped one-page text and the other is a story that has been stretched out across several pages.

▸ When anything happens in the life of the classroom, say, "We could make a story out of that!" Then you can either do a demonstration or launch every child in turning the experience into a story. To do a demonstration, just take hold of a blank book, visibly look up in the air until you get the movie of the experience in your mind, then touch page one and say the words you'd write (words that match what's in your mind), and then touch page two and continue without side comments till your story is done. You'll want to have done this a few times (in response to various classroom events) before you solicit children to do it. Alternatively, you might say to all the children, "Take hold of a booklet," and show how they can hold an imaginary booklet. "Touch the first page and say the exact words you'll write, then touch the second page. . . ."

▸ If you want to help children say and write stories which incorporate literary language, tell children that different kinds of writing have different sounds, different words. Directions sound like this: "First you need," "Then you," "Next," "Be sure to." You could ask children to listen to a little story and to tell you words story-writers use. List these: "one day," "a little later," "all of a sudden," and ask children to tell the story of some shared event to a partner, using these kinds of words.

STRETCHING AND WRITING WORDS

GETTING READY

- Wipe board, marker, and eraser (the minilesson will proceed more smoothly if children have used these tools in word study and interactive writing)
- Small Moment from your life
- Chart paper booklet, three pages long, on which you've already drawn a story (you will not need space for sentences)
- Large dry-erase board for writing
- See CD-ROM for resources

WHEN THIS UNIT IS TAUGHT EARLY IN THE YEAR, *and especially when it is taught to kindergartners or to first graders who haven't experienced a writing workshop, the unit must see-saw back and forth between work with personal narrative and work with saying words slowly, hearing and recording the sounds. You'll need to teach minilessons and small-group strategy lessons to help children learn how to put print on the page, reread their writing, leave spaces between words, and so forth.*

In this minilesson, you will again teach children the strategy of saying a word, recording the sounds the child hears, rereading what the child has written and continuing to say the remaining word, listening to the next sound, then again recording that sound, and so on. You'll model these processes as you write part of your own story. Then you will ask the children to help you write another word for your story by working on their individual wipe boards.

In this session, then, you will help writers separate out the many sounds they hear in words and write down the letters that correspond to those sounds.

THE MINILESSON

Connection

Explain to the students that writers say words they don't know slowly, writing all the sounds so that people can read their writing.

    "Writers, we have been writing these beautiful Small Moments from our lives and we want people to read them. We need to write words in such a way that people can read our stories. Writers *say the word slowly, stretching the word out, and writing all the sounds we hear*. I'll teach you how to do this, and then we can all write words that people can read."

Teaching

Open an oversized booklet to one page. Show the picture that illustrates part of a Small Moment from your life. Tell the story of this page.

    "I drew this Small Moment: 'Last night I was walking across the road, and I saw a man who fell, so I helped him up and he held my hand to thank me. He made me remember my own grandfather.'"

Demonstrate the strategies you use to write words: Say the word you want to write slowly, ever-so-slightly exaggerating the sounds. Demonstrate listening and writing the letter for the sound.

    "I want to write *man*. Watch how I do it. I'm going to listen to the sound at the beginning of *man. Man. Mm*an. /m/. Now I am going to say it slowly again and write a letter that makes the sound I hear. *M-a-n*. Oh! I hear an /m/ at the beginning." Abby wrote *m*.

Over and over again, you should notice that minlessons begin with the teacher recalling what the class has been studying, often citing a tiny example from earlier work. Then the teacher tells children today's teaching point. Generally, the teacher says, "One thing that writers do a lot is . . . and today I'll teach you to do that."

When you do this, choose a word such as man *or* Mom *or* sun *that begins with a familiar consonant and that has a few clear, distinct sounds.*

Put your finger under the letter and reread the letter you've written. Say the rest of the word, listening to the sounds that you haven't yet recorded. Repeat the process you used above.

> "Let me reread what I wrote." Abby pointed under the m, and read /m/. "/m/ /m/ m(an)."

When you or the child has written just one consonant sound for each word and it is time to read "the words," you'll face a decision. Do you want to read 'i l m m' as if it says (as the child hopes), "I like my mom," or do you want to read it so l says /l/? The answer depends on your children. If you think it will benefit them to be nudged to hear medial and/or final consonant sounds, you may want to read l as /l/ not "like." If the child has just begun hearing and recording any sounds at all, for a time you'll act as if "Wow, you are writing!" and you will read their abbreviated versions of words as if they conveyed meaning, "I like my mom!" The trick when teaching minilessons is that your class includes a range of abilities, and you'll need to decide how to aim instruction toward the bulk of the class.

Abby's children are a fairly proficient group. Most of them attended nursery school. She is aiming higher, therefore, than would some other kindergarten teachers.

> "Let me say the word slowly again. I want to hear the last sound. *M-a-n. Man. Man.* Oh! I hear /n/ /n/. That's a *n*." Abby wrote the letter *n* so now the word read *mn*.

Again put your finger under the letters and reread what you have written so far.

> "Now I think I wrote the word *man*. Let me reread it." With her finger under the print, she read it: "*Man.* Wow! It really helped me to say the word slowly and write the sounds I hear."

You will probably spell the word in a way that matches how most children can spell it if they try hard. If you are trying to write rabbit, you may reread the r as /ra/ and then set to work recording the /b/. That is, you probably won't record sounds you don't think your children will hear, but this is your judgment call. You'll make your decision based in part on the politics of your school.

Active Engagement

Ask the students to help you write another word by working on their wipe boards.

> "Now I want to write another word. I need your help to write the word *bike*." Abby showed why she needed it by pointing to her picture, "because I was on my bike when I saw the man. See if you can help me write the word *bike* beside my picture. Write *bike* on your wipe boards as we do it together."

Again, the choice of the word bike isn't an arbitrary one. The initial and final consonant sounds should be fairly accessible to most of Abby's children.

Repeat the steps you want writers to take.

"First we say the word. Watch me say the word *bike* slowly. *B-i-k-e*. Now you say the word slowly. What sound do you hear at the beginning of *bike*? Listen, and then tell your partner the first sound you hear. /b/ Write the letter that makes a /b/ sound. Put your finger under what you've written and let's read it together. /b/. We wrote /b/. We want to write *bike*. /b/ /ike/ /ike/. Say the next sound /ike/, write what you hear. Fingers under the letters and let's reread it."

Ask what they wrote on their boards, and use their help to label *your* picture.

"Will someone tell me what you wrote on your board so I can label bike on my picture?"

Maya held up her board. "I wrote *b-i-k*."

"Thanks. I'll put that on my story." Abby then wrote *bik* on the paper next to the picture of the bike.

Link

Name the strategy you used, and remind students to use this strategy in their writing from now on.

"Remember the strategy we just used. Say the word, then stretch the word out by saying it slowly, and then write one sound. *Then reread what you've written so far* (this is the key!) and again say the rest of the word slowly, listening for the next sound you hear. When you are writing your Small Moments today, try to use this strategy so that people can read your words."

They will have written different things, but right now you are coaching them through the steps of this process and this isn't the best time to fret over the right answer.

You will need to decide how you feel about writing bik *(not* bike*). I'd feel great about this, but if it matters to you, you can sneak a final* e *onto* bik *without causing any big deal. Just mutter, "Actually, this is mostly right, but there's also an* e," *and move on.*

You may choose to repeat this process by having the children write an additional label on their white boards (perhaps with less scaffolding from you) if you have time.

Notice that this minilesson doesn't set the children up for the main work they'll be doing that day. Instead, it reminds them of a strategy to incorporate as they write whatever they'll be writing. It is important that our minilessons don't always set out work for writers to do, and it is especially important that they don't set out work that requires the entire workshop. Children should be involved in ongoing work and be able to keep themselves productive without explicit instructions from you.

TIME TO CONFER

You'll continue to devote time in conferences to helping children focus in on a Small Moment, telling it in a sequential, step-by-step way across several pages. These conferences may begin with the prompt, "What are you working on as a writer?" or with the more focused question, "What are you writing about?" If a child has selected a broad swatch of time to recreate, you may ask focusing questions. "What is the most important part of your story?" Then take the child to the beginning of that selected episode and help the child envision the start of the episode by making a movie in his or her mind. "How did it start? What happened first?" If the child's retelling of the episode continues to be full of generalizations, elicit more specifics. "So what exactly did she say?" or "What exactly did you do?" Those two questions allow you to elicit a story from the writer. Say the story back to the child in a narrative form, as you turn the pages. "So, am I right that your story goes like this . . . ?" Don't elicit a ten-page long novel if the child can write only a five-line narrative! See the conferences cited at right from the *Conferring with Primary Writers* book.

While teaching children to see their lives as full of stories, you'll also want to help children with the print work of writing. You'll need to adjust your support so that you set up one child to label her drawing, another to write a one-line sentence under each picture, and yet another to write paragraphs on each of several pages in a booklet. Small-group strategy lessons are essential.

These conferences in *The Conferring Handbook* may be especially helpful today:

▶ *"Will You Touch Each Page and Say What You'll Write?"*
▶ *"Let Me Help You Put Some Words Down"*
▶ *"As a Reader, I'd Love to Hear More About That"*

Also, if you have *Conferring with Primary Writers*, you may want to refer to the following conference:

▶ "But How Did You *Get* There?!"
▶ "Is This a Story About Your Life?"
▶ "Can I Show You How to Write What Happened, First, Then Next, Then Next?"

Call the children on to the rug. Have a writer come up and explain how he stretched out words.

"Hey writers, let's come together. Eyes on Keo: He has something so cool to tell us about his writing work today. Keo, tell us what happened when you were writing *road* today."

"First I wrote *r* for *road*," Keo said, making the *r* on a wipe board. "But then I read it and it didn't say *road*!" He looked surprised.

"What did it say, Keo?"

"It said '*r- r-*'. So I just stretched out the rest to make it say *road*, see, 'ROAD!'" He had written *r-o-d*.

"Isn't that cool? Keo reminded me how important it is to reread our writing as we go on to make sure we're putting down *all* of the sounds that we hear, not just one sound in a word."

Ask students to reread their work to their partners, asking themselves: Did I record all the sounds I can?

"Right now, will each of you reread your work to your partner? Put one person's booklet between you and your partner. And writers, read your story aloud pointing at the words. Check that each of you has put down all the sounds you heard. Then talk about the story, just like you talk about books when you finish reading them in the reading workshop. Then switch to the other writer's booklet."

It's crucial to remember that the share needs to be instructive to each of the listeners and not just the child who catches a moment in the spotlight, I ask the class to hear about Keo's important work because I'm trying to teach the class that I hope they, too, do as Keo has done.

Notice my enthusiasm for hearing and recording sounds. I'm hoping to make this into a cool, fun thing to do.

Be sure to have partners working together. You've instituted the structure. Now, for a time, you need to spotlight it.

Do the same minilesson again (with minor variations). This time, you can recruit the class to help you label your picture. Next time, you could teach the class that often you decide to write a sentence under the picture. Show the class that you tape a strip of paper containing a few lines onto the bottom of the page and that you remember what happened first and say that. Then show the class how you say it again and this time think, "So what word do I write first?" Write a portion of the sentence in front of the class, perhaps angling this to show that you often reread with your finger under whatever you've written. Then recruit the class to help you add on to what you've written. You'll want to do small group strategy lessons and conferences to help children begin to write conventionally.

One day you can focus on learning and recording beginning sounds, another day on ending or medial sounds. Other days, you can stress the importance of children rereading the letters they've recorded and then continuing to write. The next book in the series, *Writing for Readers*, contains many minilessons geared to help children write more conventionally. You may want to import one or two of these minilessons into this unit, or use variations of these minilessons as small group strategy lessons.

Some days when you check in on the work your writers have been doing, you'll focus on their most recent work, looking especially at the texts that are still under construction (in the green-dot section of the child's folder). Other times, you'll want to survey all the work that a few (or all) of your children have done. It helps to literally spread out on the table all the work one child has done, starting on day one of the unit. You should see evidence of a lot of productivity. Some children will write a booklet each day, some will spend two days on a booklet. Either way, by now each child should have written several stories. Those stories should contain a fair amount of writing, too.

You can almost count on the fact that some children will have produced less than you'd like to see. Usually this is because the child is devoting a large percentage of time to coloring in the sky and the grass in the landscapes and to adding buttons and lacework onto the outfits. You have probably known all along that some children's drawings were more elaborate than you would have liked to see, but at the start of the year, the fact that kids were drawing as well as writing during the writing workshop provided you with immeasurable help maintaining a productive, workman-like hum in the workshop. By now, however, your children's abilities to write and their stamina with writing should be stronger, and you probably have more things under control. So you will want to decrease the amount of time children spend on their illustrations so as to turn the flame up under their writing. One way to do this is to switch from marker pens in a range of colors to writing and drawing with a single marker pen. To soften that transition, some teachers provide writers with special new pens and call them "writers' pens." Some teachers just have some, not all, children "graduate" to the place where they use "writing pens" (and sketch but do not color-in their pictures).

SKETCHING RATHER THAN DRAWING

GETTING READY

- Piece of paper
- Booklet of chart paper
- Markers for drawing and sketching
- Chart that lists three steps to writing: sketch, write words, and add color and details
- Pencil
- See CD-ROM for resources

WHEN, IN THE PROCESS OF ASSESSMENT, *Abby and I categorized her children as writers, we found that two of her writers were either not writing or were writing in seemingly random strings of letters. These children needed to be encouraged to label their drawings more. Six others needed help focusing their stories. Another half a dozen seemed as if they'd profit from instruction in the qualities of good writing. A fairly large group wasn't spending enough time actually writing. When teachers do this sort of categorization, we come to school ready to do a lot of conferring and small-group work.*

Abby and I were especially concerned about the children who were drawing such intricate pictures that they didn't have much time left over for writing. We decided to turn this concern into a minilesson. Instead of scolding children for not writing, Abby taught them a way to draw more efficiently so that luckily they'd have more of a chance to write! Specifically, she demonstrated that when she uses sketching (not drawing) to help her prepare for writing, she has time enough to write a lot of words.

This session will teach the difference between sketching and drawing, emphasizing that sketching is appropriate in the writing workshop so we can reserve time for writing.

THE MINILESSON

Connection

Tell your children that when you read their work after school, you found some work that had great pictures but alas, had hardly any words!

"Last night I brought all your work to my study group at Teachers College. I filled the table with your work and we all looked over your pieces and read your stories. But you know what? Sometimes we'd pull a piece out of the pile, and it'd have a picture that made us dying to read the story, then we'd turn to find the words, and, and, and. . . ." Here Abby reenacted someone searching for words, looking high and low through the pages of a booklet for words, "and there would be *almost no* words!" Abby's voice made this sound like a tragedy indeed. "I realized some of you have been working SO hard at making detailed, colorful illustrations that you ran out of time to write words!" Abby looked shocked and sad over this glum state of affairs.

Tell your children you will teach a strategy that will help them make time for the words.

"Today I'm going to teach you a special kind of drawing that writers use when we want to save time for writing. We call it *sketching*."

Teaching

Using your own Small Moment story, demonstrate the difference between sketching and drawing.

"We can use this special strategy, *sketching*, to help us have time to write our words and draw our stories."

"I'm going to show you the difference between drawing and sketching. Watch, and I'll first *draw* my baby nephew. I'll pick yellow for his crib," she muttered and started to carefully draw a crib. Then she added her nephew, switching markers to show his brown curly hair and a blue zip-up suit. "Now I better put his bedroom because I'm drawing, I want to put it all down." At this point she stepped out of her role.

Abby's children love learning that their teacher goes to school too. They especially love the idea that teachers from across the city meet at a college to study their work. This makes Abby's five-year-olds feel special.

The message of a writing workshop is this: Each of us is a writer, and we can write just like the writers we love—Mem Fox, Bill Martin, and the others. Teachers often extend this message to teach particular points. "Let me show you how writers store our work. As writers, we keep our work in portfolios and . . . ." "Did you know that writers go to lunch differently than people who aren't writers? It's true! Because writers are always thinking. I could write about that!"

Turning to the other side of the page, Abby set up a contrast. "Now watch me *sketch*," she said, and with a pencil and a few bold lines she outlined a crib, baby (represented by a head and an oval body), and chair. Within a minute, she was done.

Return to the chart from earlier, in which you listed the steps involved in writing a Small Moment story. Show children how you revised the chart.

"Writers sketch," Abby said and pointed to the icon accompanying this item, "so we still have time to write. You can sketch each page, write your words, and then maybe go back and add color and detail." Abby again pointed to and read from the chart on her easel. Each item also had an icon to make the worda understandable:

WRITING SMALL MOMENTS

* Writers think of something that happened to them.
* They picture it in their mind.
* They sketch it on the paper.
* They write words on each page.
* They add color and detail.

Raphael bounced on his knees waving his thumb in the air, "Can I tell you something? A sketch is a picture with just a pencil. It is like really fast," and he proceeded to run his hands back and forth quickly to show the rapidity of a sketch.

"Exactly, Raphael. A sketch is just a quick drawing. We will *sketch* our stories with pencils. You don't add the details in a sketch. The sketch just holds your story on the page."

This minilesson is vastly more effective because we watch Abby actually go about making the two alternative versions. The minilesson would not have worked as well had she merely held up a completed drawing and a completed sketch and talked about the differences. When we intend to make a point, it often helps to present children with examples that are so extreme they are almost caricatures.

Charts in a primary writing workshop are always sparse and usually illustrated with icons. It is not okay to have instructional charts that at least a third of the class can't access.

Abby doesn't want her children to blurt out as Raphael has just done, and she certainly doesn't encourage this. If she did, half a dozen kids would interject into every minilesson. But even without encouraging these interjections, they happen. Sometimes they are totally off subject. Raphael could have said, "Don't you know, you just give the fish a tiny pinch of food or they get too fat and die." Had he said this, Abby would have said, "Raphael, this isn't the time to talk about fish. This is time for the minilesson and I'm teaching you." If Raphael often interjects with pertinent additions as he's done now, Abby will still need to let him (and others) know her ground rules. "Raphael, that is a smart comment but this is the part of the minilesson where I talk to you. Your job right now is to listen and to think, but not to talk. In a minute, you'll have a chance to talk."

Show them how you sketch on each page and then write your story on each page.

"Watch me do my writing," Abby held up a booklet and acted out an obvious thinking phase. "Oh!" she said, clearly deciding on her topic. Now she touched the first page. "I am going to write, 'Last night I couldn't sleep.'" Turning to touch the second page, she said, "'I got up and read for a while.'" Turning the page again, "'I fell asleep with my book on my face!'"

"Now I'm going to sketch my story," Abby muttered, as if speaking to herself. With a few quick strokes, she illustrated each page. She stopped midway through the second page and made a comment to the children. "Did you notice I'm not even giving myself hair or eyes? I can add those details later." Finishing the third page, she said, "Now I'm ready to do my writing," and soon she'd returned to page one and labeled *me, bed,* and made a speech bubble full of snoring *z*'s.

As she finished labeling page one, Abby said, "After I write on pages two and three, I'll add color and details."

Abby stopped in the midst of her demonstration and said, "I am going to let you begin your writing now."

Active Engagement

Ask the students to picture in their minds what they'll write, and then what they'll sketch, not draw.

"Before you go, think about what you are going to do as a writer today. Thumbs up when you know what you will be writing about." The room was silent for a moment, and soon most of the children had signaled they knew their topic. "Okay now, listen. This will be hard. Pretend you have your booklet in front of you. Open it to page one and whisper what you'll write, or what you have already written if you already started the book. Then turn to the next pretend page, touch that page and say in a whisper, what you'll write on that page. Then finish the story. When you've said the words, go back to page one and, with your finger, start sketching. On your pretend book—put what you will sketch. Keep going till I tell you to stop."

Notice the nice trim nature of this story. Abby's point in this minilesson is to show how she sketches all three pages, says the story for all three pages, and only then begins to write. In order to make this point, she probably profits from a very lean story. The best thing about her story is it celebrates an ordinary everyday moment. Better yet, it shows Abby as an avid reader!

Abby chooses to label her drawing because some of her children were doing this when they wrote, and these were the very children who especially needed support.

The words Abby chooses, "I'm going to let you begin your writing," convey important assumptions. She acts as if they are of course dying to get a chance to write.

Children love to pretend. How wise to take advantage of this in your active engagement.

Link

Send them off, reminding them to take this lesson with them.

After a bit, Abby moved among them as they worked, touching shoulders and signaling, "Off you go," to individuals. "Remember to do this same thing today and every day when you write."

MID-WORKSHOP TEACHING POINT

Ask children to check in with their partners about the amount of writing they have done so far.

"Writers, would you get with your partner? I want you to show each other how much writing you've gotten done today. Did you write more words than yesterday? Partners, if your friend hasn't gotten much writing done, be a teacher for your friend and say, 'You *gotta* write!' Help your friend get started putting some words down, okay?"

Teachers sometimes have trouble organizing tiny interludes of active involvement such as this one. Bear in mind that one idea such as this one can be used on dozens of occasions. If you want to teach children to stretch out, listen to, and spell a word, they can write with pretend pens on a pretend wipe-board.

You have no choice but to continue to use the partnership structure now that you've launched it, if you believe in it. In time, it can be a structure you use often, but not always, but for now you'll want to keep a spotlight on partnerships so that they will work well.

TIME TO CONFER

By now, you'll have a whole repertoire of possible conferences. As you listen in on what a child is doing and saying, you can use the conferring checklist for this unit to remind you of topics you could teach. You'll think, as you listen to a child, "Am I going to do a focus conference?" or "Will this be an 'instead of labels, you might want to write sentences' conference?" Sometimes your conferences will be, "Writers don't waste precious writing time." Today's minilesson will probably steer you towards a few "sketch instead of draw conferences" like the one with Ethan.

By now, your unit of study should be well enough launched that you can give special attention to writers who need a boost. When working with children who concern you, it's crucial to let your assessment steer what you do. If a first grader isn't yet making any sound-symbol correspondences, for example, my teaching with this child will touch lightly on the importance of stretching a story out across several pages, but the focus of my attention will be on helping this child understand that words have component sounds, that the sounds can be isolated and recorded by means of letters. My goal for this child will be for the child to make steady progress in this important dimension. Therefore, for a stretch of days, I'll try to return to the child every day, working consistently and repeatedly on teaching this child to stretch words out, to listen for and isolate the first sound (this is phonemic awareness), and to know a few consonant letters and use these to record the sounds the child hears at the start of some words. With daily support, a child can learn to label parts of his or her drawings. If the child has worked with the letter *m*, I'll ask her to record sounds in ways that label herself (me), her mom, and so on, and I'll expect several *m*'s to dot her drawing. See "Let Me Help You Put Some Words Down" in part two and part three from the *Conferring with Primary Writers* book.

These conferences in *The Conferring Handbook* may be especially helpful today:

▶ *"Will You Touch Each Page and Say What You'll Write?"*

▶ *"Let Me Help You Put Some Words Down"*

▶ *"As a Reader, I'd Love to Hear More About That"*

Also, if you have *Conferring with Primary Writers*, you may want to refer to the following conferences:

▶ "Writers Make Time to Write Words"

▶ "Let Me Help You Put Some Words Down"

AFTER-THE-WORKSHOP SHARE

Call the children to the rug. Tell them about a writer in the class who returned to an earlier piece and wrote more words.

"Writers, I saw so many people writing words today! Thumbs up if you had more time to write words today because you sketched first. Wow!"

"When Jason and I were talking about his writing, he noticed that the piece he began yesterday was in a booklet with three pages, and that he had drawn this beautiful picture full of details and color on the first page, but that he hadn't included *any* words. And he had spent so much time on page one, he had *nothing at all* on the middle or the last page! Jason, can you tell us what your idea was for how to make sure you got to the words today?"

"Well I just sketched it, the rest of the story, when I unwrapped the Lego castle in the living room, and when I put it together with my dad."

"Wow! So you got the idea to sketch, not draw!" I said as if this was a revelation. "Did that give you a chance to write more words?" Jason nodded proudly. "Can you show us your words, Jason?" Jason had labeled several elements of his picture on each page.

He read, "*Me, box, Lego, castle*, and *Dad*."

"And Jason, will you tell the kids what you did with page one, the page you thought was finished?"

"I went back and added words."

"Isn't that cool? And now Jason is looking through old writing he did *even earlier in the year* to see if he can add words to any of it! Isn't this amazing? I'm definitely going to tell my friends at Teachers College about Jason's brilliant idea."

Tell children that maybe some of them will go back and add words on pieces. Ask them to tell partners what they've learned.

"Maybe some of you, like Jason, will *go back* and add words or add pictures to earlier writing! Tell your partner what you've learned today that you'll carry with you always."

This is a nice reminder that the whole reason to sketch, not draw, is that writers want to save time for words.

You'll notice that in some share sessions, the teacher tells the story of a particular child's work and in other share sessions, the teacher turns "the microphone" over to the child as I do in this instance. I still preface and re-state what Jason says because I want to make sure to extrapolate out a teaching point that pertains to the entire class.

Notice my assumption that Jason is dying to find a way to "get the chance to write more words."

When a child learns to do something and does it once on today's piece of writing, a wonderful way to be sure the child gets lots of practice using that strategy is to suggest the child reread previously finished pieces, searching for more places where the child could employ the strategy.

PLANNING DETAILS

GETTING READY

▶ Selected, focused vignette from the class' recent, everyday life
▶ Booklet of chart paper and marker
⦿ See CD-ROM for resources

IN THE PRECEDING SESSION, YOU PROMPTED YOUR STUDENTS *to get more words down in their stories by making fast sketches rather than time-consuming pictures. Now you'll shift your spotlight to the words themselves and encourage children to tell and write detailed, focused stories. Specifically, you'll help children to use their partnerships as a forum for planning stories that are designed from the start to be detailed narratives. This is a sensible subject for this session because the partners, above all, are planning together. This minilesson lifts the level of those newly established partnerships.*

In this session, you will encourage children to plan detailed stories by saying detailed stories aloud before beginning to write them.

The Minilesson

Connection

Celebrate that your children have been adding details into their Small Moment stories. Tell them that today they will help _you_ include details in _your_ writing.

"Last night at home I kept remembering the other day when we read Sam's piece. Remember how he wrote not only that he saw big dinosaurs but _that he touched one with his hand_. That's a detail all of us remember, and we can picture Sam touching that dinosaur, can't we? And remember the details from Nicholas' book, when his friend gave him a hug that hurt in the middle and he said to his friend, 'Jonathan that's enough' until he stopped? What details! We remember these details just like we remember that on her way home, Vera Williams walked past yellow and red tulips. What details! Today I hope you can help me be sure the story I write is one that has beautiful details, too. And I hope that you'll learn that writers plan our stories so as to be sure we include details."

Qualities of good writing are also qualities of good teaching. Details matter not only in pieces of writing but also in our teaching. These opening comments are far more memorable because Abby uses not only a general imperative, "write with details," but also uses tiny particulars to make her point, referring back to Sam touching the dinosaur with his hand, to Nicholas' book about the hug that hurt in the middle, and to Vera seeing yellow and red tulips. Although Abby is explicitly teaching children that details matter, she is also conveying to them that their stories matter, that they leave a lasting impression on her.

Notice that minilessons often revisit the same stories over and over, each time highlighting a different aspect of the story. When you make reference to a story often, as Abby is doing with Vera Williams' A Chair for My Mother, you will probably want to be sure the story is very alive in every child's mind (including the child who was absent or absentminded on earlier days), and so you'll probably reread the story (for sheer pleasure more than to illustrate specific teaching points) at another time of day.

Teaching

Remind the class of a shared experience in all its richness. Then plan how you might write about that experience. Touch each empty page and say aloud a bare-bones version of the story.

"Remember how we had that fire drill the other day? Well, I want to write about it because I keep remembering how we walked down the warm hall, then pushed open the door and suddenly it was so cold. We were hopping up and down to keep warm."

When you are in front of the class recalling an episode, act out the writing process so that you actually recall the episode as you talk. After you say, "Remember how we had that fire drill?" (that is, after you name whatever you remember), pause. Let your eyes get a faraway look and actually recall the episode. Then when you say the details you recall, such as, "I keep remembering how we walked down the warm hall, then pushed open the door . . ." the children will be with you. Speak so that as you talk, it's clear from your intonation that you are remembering (for example) shoving at that door and the blast of cold air that followed. Shiver!

"So if I was planning my story with my partner—Felecia, would you be my partner please?—I'm going to write," Abby touched the first page as she said, "'We heard the fire drill.'" She turned the page and touched the next page. "'We went outside.'" Again, she turned the page and touched the next one, saying, "'We came in.'"

Clearly this story leaves out most of the wonderful details. Don't hesitate to create an extreme example that drives home your point.

Let children listen in as you muse aloud over whether your story has details.

Abby acted puzzled as she put her hands to her chin, "Huh, I wrote a Small Moment about the fire drill, but I am wondering, did I add enough details to give a clear picture what the fire drill was like? Hmm. . . ." She repeated the story, as if musing over whether or not her story was detailed. "'We heard a fire drill. We went outside. We came in.'"

Again, this only works because Abby is willing to be dramatic. She gets the kids started mulling over the question of whether her sparse story is detailed because she starts mulling over this in front of them, then leaves off in a way that allows them to continue.

Miles, with his perfect posture, said, "Well, you forgot to say how cold it was and stuff."

Abby replied excitedly, "Yeah, I did forget a lot of details! I said what happened, but I didn't give you readers any details to help you get a clear picture."

Let your intonation suggest that the child just helped you rather than that the child just succeeded in saying what you'd been waiting for someone to say.

Active Engagement

Ask the students to tell their partners some details you could add to improve the story. Listen in on the partnership talks.

"Since we were all a part of this Small Moment at the fire drill, could you talk to your partner and suggest details I could have included that would have made my story better?"

Camilla: "Abby should say how when we opened the door to go out it was like an ice cube!"

Jorge: "I didn't want to go out."

Reconvene the group after about two minutes, asking them which details they think should be included.

"I heard a lot of really important details I could add to make my story better. Will someone share a detail they think I should add?"

Hanna Joy: "You should say that we are all smushed up to the other class and how it was so cold!"

Miles: "We were out there for so long."

Isabella: "We didn't have our jackets because we were at lunch when the bell gonged."

"What important details for me to include! Thank you writers. Let me try again to plan out my story. So, Felecia, you're my partner. I'm going to write," Abby touched the first page, "'We heard the fire drill. We pushed the door to go outside but it was like an ice cube out there. We didn't want to go out but we did.'" Abby turned the page. "'We didn't have jackets on so it was cold but we smushed up to another class to get warmer. Finally we could go back in.' That's better, isn't it?"

It's much more realistic to ask children to think of details that could be added into this fire drill story than it would be to suggest each child retrieve his or her writing from the day before, reread it, or decide whether it needs more details. Some children will disperse to their writing nooks with their folders in hand and that's the perfect time to transfer your lesson to each particular case. During the minilesson, it's vastly more efficient for children to pitch in ideas for remedying the fire drill story.

If we use the marker to actually add the details into the text itself during the minilesson, this slows the minilesson down and keeps children on the rug too long. Children learn mostly from their own work writing, and therefore we need to keep minilessons less than ten minutes. Later, after school, you can take the notes you have scrawled on your clipboard and use them to help you make the anticipated changes to the text.

Link

Remind the class of the growing repertoire of guidelines they've developed together.

"When you begin stories, remember all the things we've been talking about in our study of Small Moments. You'll want to think of something that happened to you, picture it in your mind, and then, before you write, tell your partner the story with all the details. Plan together how your story will go. Then you can sketch and write it across the pages. Thumbs up if you think you can do all those things! Great! If you are at the red table, go reread your folders and get started."

Your most important job during the link is to restate the teaching point in a way that puts it into the context of children's ongoing writing work. But often you will do this by showing children that today's lesson adds to their growing repertoire of strategies.

Time to Confer

Although your minilessons lately have not focused on the importance of hearing and recording sounds, rereading what one has written, or leaving spaces between words, you'll devote a fair proportion of your conference and strategy lesson time to this work. Remember to let your children do most of the work. When teachers say to me, "My kids keep asking for spelling help," I respond, "That's because you keep giving it." Don't let yourself become a walking dictionary. If a child says, "How do you spell *dinosaur*?" say, "You know how to tackle a word like that, don't you? What do writers do first when they want to spell a word?" The child *should* know, by now, the process of getting a word down on paper. If not, that should be your conference, of course.

You'll repeat this work with letters and sounds often. In a kindergarten class, you'll probably help children write words in at least one-third of your conferences. In your first-grade classrooms, children should be more self-reliant at this, but you'll need to remind them to use high-frequency words, to incorporate word endings, to write with punctuation, and so forth.

These conferences in *The Conferring Handbook* may be especially helpful today:

▶ *"Will You Touch Each Page and Say What You'll Write?"*
▶ *"Let Me Help You Put Some Words Down"*
▶ *"As a Reader, I'd Love to Hear More About That"*

Also, if you have *Conferring with Primary Writers*, you may want to refer to the conferences in part three.

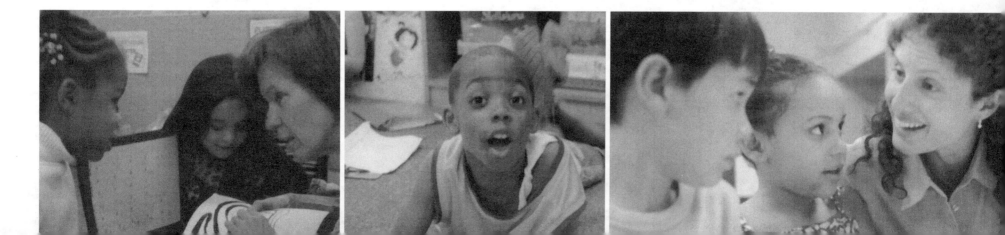

At the end of the writing time, call the class back to the meeting area for a share. Ask two students who have written stories with details to share.

"Alexa has written a piece about last Christmas, and she wrote with tiny details. Listen." [*Fig. VII-1*]

Extol the details, showing how these help you as a reader.

"I love the way Alexa gave us details from her Small Moment. She told us about how when she saw the package, it was big and heavy. Then she tore a tiny bit of the paper and saw inside. And finally she'd opened the package and was holding a brand-new doll! What a story. I have a really good picture in my mind of what that must have been like. I feel like I was there. Would each of you read your story with your partner and notice the details you have included?"

It was Christmas Eve. I had a heavy, big package.

I tore the big package. I peeked inside it (and) saw plastic and a doll.

I opened the package. It was a doll. I put her on my lap. It was my favorite doll.

Fig. VII-1   Alexa

The need to teach children to write with detail never goes away. Even when I work with college students, the biggest issue with their writing is it is underdeveloped. As you develop minilessons that teach children to write with detail, here are a few suggestions:

- It helps to show a contrast. Contrast a bare-bones draft that you or a child wrote with a more detailed and focused version of the same story.

- Rather than simply showing that one version is better than another because the one is detailed, reenact the process of writing with detail so children learn not only the importance, but also the process of writing with detail.

- You might show an excerpt of a published text that contains details. "This author probably first wrote," and then produce a bare-bones version of the same text. "Then he (or she) probably reread it and decided. . . ."

- Aim for honest, precise details. A favorite of mine is Cynthia Rylant's description of trying to sleep in a house full of relatives. "It was hard going to sleep with all that new breathing in the house."

- Retell the good work you saw a child doing. Show aspects of the child's process that you want the class to emulate. "Let me tell you how Tashika wrote her Small Moment yesterday. First, she thought of what she could write about. She said, 'Hmmm . . . Maybe I could write about all the fun things I do after school.' Then she decided, 'No! I'm going to write about just one thing.'" When you select children to use as mentors, choose less as well as more proficient writers.

- Engage the class in shared writing about a small, everyday occurrence. "Remember how we came back from gym and our room was locked and I couldn't find the keys? Why don't we write about that? First, we need to remember exactly what happened, so turn your brains on. Take a minute to remember. What happened first, then next. Tell your partner." They would. "Who can suggest a way to start this story?"

INTERNALIZING STORY SHAPES

GETTING READY

▶ Story of your own that you will tell across your fingers

▶ Tape or some way to affix extra sheets onto ongoing writing pages

◉ See CD-ROM for resources

AS YOU LOOK OVER YOUR CHILDREN'S WRITING, it will probably be clear to you that some of them don't yet have a real feel for a story. Some are writing commentary on subjects—"I had pizza. It was good. I like pizza."—in lieu of telling stories. And some children are listing rather than developing stories—"My cat runs. My cat sleeps. My cat purrs."

As these children listen to more and more stories, those that are told to them and those that are read aloud, the texts these children write will take on the rhythms and design of stories. Try to find many, many occasions for shared stories including times when stories are read to and told to these particular children in small groups. Meanwhile, you want new ways to convey a sense of story to kids. In the prelude to this book, we describe the way Natalie Louis (the coauthor of our upcoming unit Writing for Readers) inducted her children into a storytelling culture. She and her class told and retold the story of their trip to the firehouse. She also helped children find stories in the details of their recess play, and she urged them to catch those stories in their hands and to tell the stories across their fingers. Children will learn that their fingers can act as graphic organizers, helping them to tell stories that have beginnings, middles, and endings. In this lesson, you'll bring Natalie's idea to your children.

In this session you teach children the strategy of telling a story across their fingers to help them produce stories that have a beginning, middle, and end.

THE MINILESSON

Connection

Tell the children that, as writers, we find stories in everyday occurrences and hold these stories in our hands, writing them later.

"I can tell that you, like me, are seeing stories everywhere. Yesterday Brian finished a story and was handing it to me. But his paper slipped out of his hand and floated like a magic carpet, down, down, and flew right inside the trash can. Brian and I realized that what had just happened—him saying, 'I'm done!' and then dropping his story, and it floating down and landing in the trash— could make *another* story! He said, 'I could write a story about that.' Brian was exactly right, and I told him, 'Catch that story idea, then.' Today I'm going to show you a way writers catch story ideas. When Brian realized, 'Wait, this could make a story!' he could catch the idea like this." Abby reached out as if she could catch Brian's story in her hand and then shoved her hand, still holding the story, into her pocket. Pulling her hand out, Abby patted the pocket with pleasure. "Writers do that. We find stories everywhere in our lives, and we hold onto them," she said, again gesturing as if she were reaching for and holding onto a story, "until we can write them down."

Teaching

Demonstrate taking a story out of your pocket (fist tight) and then telling your story by raising one finger for each part of the story.

"Then, later, you can always reach your hand into your pocket and take out a story. And you have a story-helper, too, because you pull your story out like this," Abby reached into her pocket and pulled out a fist. "Watch how I tell a story across my fingers."

In today's minilesson, you will try to give children another chance to grasp the big idea of this unit.

Above all, you want your children to begin to tell and write stories. Some children find this easy because they grow up in homes in which stories are constantly told and read. But some children rely on schools as the place to learn about narratives. It's important to help every child understand that with words, we can create a world, and recreate the drama of life within that world. In this minilesson, you give children a physical, embodied way to understand the rhythm of stories.

Abby raised her thumb, "I was running in a race through the park." Abby then raised her second finger, "A lot of people were passing me." She raised her third finger and continued, "And then I saw the finish line." She said in an aside to the class, "I better start finishing my story. I only have two more fingers!" Then she held up her fourth finger, with only one finger remaining closed and said, "I ran through the finish line and raised my arms up." She slowly raised her last finger and said with a wrapping-up tone of voice, "'I hugged my mother and sister who were waiting at the finish line.' Did you see how I told one part of my story on each finger?"

Sophia raised her hand, "Can I have my cough drop? My mom said I can only have three," as she raised up three fingers in Abby's view, "or I will overdose."

"Sophia, this doesn't have to do with what we are talking about right now. Let's talk about your cough drops later."

Active Engagement

Tell your children to think of what they are going to write about, and then ask them to tell their stories across their fingers, to their partners.

"Now I want you to catch a Small Moment in your minds and in one of your hands. Think of what you are writing about." Abby paused to give her children thinking time. "You got it?" she held her closed fist out again. Most of the children copied her. "Now turn to your partner, try and tell your moment using your fingers. Remember that when you only have one or two fingers left, this is a sign that you should be finishing your story."

The students turned to their partners and began to tell their stories using their fingers. As Abby listened in, she heard Katherine say, raising her first finger, "I went to the beach." She raised her second finger. "I played in the ocean." She raised her third finger. "I was splashing my dad." Her fourth finger went up. "We put the shovels in the car." She stuck up her thumb and ended, "We went home."

We need to find every imaginable way to bring home to children the central concepts we are trying to teach. This graphic illustrator is a perfect way to help children develop an internalized sense for the shape of a story, and it will mean a lot to some children, and especially to those who have difficulty when all our instructions rely on verbal communications.

The idea of telling a story across one's fingers came from Natalie Louis, and the truth is that lots of these minilessons rely on ideas that emerged only because a group of teachers and I were in a study group together. Remember that one of the best ways to invent beautiful teaching is to plan your teaching in the company of others!

These interruptions are bound to happen—be ready to not only stay the course of your minilesson but also to teach children that they are expected to stay on the subject of the minilesson.

Don't underestimate the value of actually pausing. Watch your children's eyes and wait until you can see that they recall their stories.

Share the work of a child who told her story well as reinforcement of your teaching.

"Listen to how Juliana caught her Small Moment and told it with her fingers." Juliana stood up. "Eyes on Juliana," Abby whispered. Juliana repeated her story to the class.

Link

Suggest to the children that if they begin a new piece, it might help them to tell the story across their fingers first.

"You just told your moments across your fingers. If you are writing a new piece today, try planning the story across your five fingers and see if this helps you make sure you have a beginning and a middle and an end."

As you confer today, help children tell their stories across their fingers or their pages, remembering that either scaffold works in a similar way.

You'll also want to look to see which children are labeling their pictures in ways that suggest they could be writing sentences. If a child hears beginning and ending sounds in words (and especially if a child hears beginning, medial, and ending sounds), there is no reason why that child can't be writing sentences. Gather a group of these kids together, bring tape and a small pile of three-inch-wide strips of paper containing two lines, and begin by telling these children you have gathered them together because they are ready to move on from just labeling to also writing lines. "Congratulations," you'll say. "You are ready to write a whole story. I'll help you." Then help each child frame a relatively straightforward sentence. (If the sentence starts with "Whenever," for example, tinker with it a tiny bit and say it in such a way that it'll be easier to write.) Then stay with the children as they write, reminding them to say words slowly, to listen for sounds, to reread often with their fingers under the print, to leave spaces between their words, and so on. Remember as you do this that your aim is not perfection but independence. Help children to feel resourceful, competent, and confident.

These conferences in *The Conferring Handbook* may be especially helpful today:

- ▶ *"Will You Touch Each Page and Say What You'll Write?"*
- ▶ *"Let Me Help You Put Some Words Down"*
- ▶ *"As a Reader, I'd Love to Hear More About That"*

Also, if you have *Conferring with Primary Writers*, you may want to refer to the conferences in part two.

AFTER-THE-WORKSHOP SHARE

Share a conference you had with a child who added more to a story. Share the strategy you offered that child for doing this work—in this case, adding more paper for a long story.

"I was conferring with Sophie today and she wrote this wonderful story about our friendship flag." I read it [*Fig. VIII-1*] aloud.

"Then we talked about what details she could add to let the reader know even more. Sophie said 'But I don't have any more lines.' Well, writers you can add more words by taking lines," Abby showed them a one-quarter piece of paper with two or three lines on it, "and taping them where you want to write more words. This strategy helped Sophie, and it can help you also. Listen to how Sophie's story sounds now. She added more details into her drawing (she added an alphabet chart and our library) and she added more words on one page and a whole new page!" Abby read the new versions with the additions. "So writers, from now on, you can add lines when you have more to say, and in this way you can give the readers more of a picture, just like Sophie has done." [*Fig. VIII-2*]

It is yesterday when it was choice time. I was staring at them when they were making the flag.

Then I went over to them and watched. It looked so pretty.

It was clean up. It is all done.

Fig. VIII-1   Sophie

Then I went over to them and watched. It looked so pretty.
Now it is so pretty.

It had police officers and firefighters and hearts and two suns.
Now it is a friendship flag.

Fig. VIII-2   Sophie

IF CHILDREN NEED MORE TIME

- You could try some shared stories in which the class works together to retell a classroom-life vignette with each child adding a new fingerful of story! Remind children when the story needs to turn toward an ending. "We don't have many more fingers, so our story needs to end soon."

- You could read aloud a bunch of children's stories, written by members of the class, and ask children to listen across their fingers. In this way, you'll help your children internalize how their hands can be graphic organizers for stories.

- You could retell a book your children know well using one's fingers to hold the story. You and your children will come to sense that in more developed stories, each finger holds a paragraph not a sentence (not that you tell them this in these words!).

- Keep in mind that you have the option of deciding that this whole concept confuses rather than supports your children. If this is true, abandon it! The turn-of-the page in premade booklets essentially accomplishes the same job. You may decide that you'll give up on encouraging children to tell stories across their five fingers, but that instead you'll be sure all your premade booklets have five pages (rather than three) plus a cover.

- Your children may profit from a list of words that storytellers use when they progress from one part (one finger) of a story to another part. Instead of relying only on the transition "and," teach children to use phrases such as "a little later," "soon after that," "before long," "later," or "finally."

STORYTELLING WITH PARTNERS

GETTING READY

▶ Students arranged on rug next to their writing partners

▶ Story to tell the class that includes a Small Moment of something true that happened to you recently

▶ Booklet of a story you already wrote (this will be the same story you tell)

○ See CD-ROM for resources

THE WORK IN THE PRECEDING SESSION *with storytelling across one's fingers probably raised the level of children's writing in important ways. Another way to support story language and structure in your children's writing is to encourage children to tell stories to each other. If any person is given the chance to tell a story to a rapt listener, the storyteller often rises to the occasion and embellishes the story. One of the best ways to nudge children to write with literary language, then, is to create occasions for them to tell stories to others.*

In the preceding session, you encouraged children to tell stories across their fingers to their partners. The emphasis was on the storytelling-across-one's-fingers part of this. Now you'll revisit this, but you'll spotlight the role of partners.

In this session, children will practice telling stories across their fingers to their partners and the purpose of this will be to coax more literary language and elaboration out of the storytellers.

THE MINILESSON

Connection

Tell children that you are going to teach them how to tell stories with a partner.

"Writers, yesterday I watched you telling your stories across your fingers to your partners and I realized that I never taught you how to be great storytelling partners for each other. Today, I'm going to teach you how to be great writing partners."

"There are two things to learn. The first is how to do a good job when it is your turn to tell a story. The next is how to do a good job when it is your turn to listen."

Teaching

Teach children that instead of summarizing the story they plan to write, they should say the actual words of the story.

"When you are telling your partner your story, what some of you do is (I gestured for Felecia to join me and asked her to pretend to be my partner) you say to your partner, 'I'm going to write all about visiting my cousin. I'll tell what we did, the picnic and all.'"

"It's *much more helpful* if instead, you say the actual words that you plan to write. So I wouldn't say to Felecia, 'I'm going to write all about visiting my cousin. I'll tell what we did, the picnic and all.' Instead I say this to her:"

> Nan and I started to eat sandwiches in the garden. We were laughing and talking. Then a raindrop landed on my hand. We didn't want to go in but we did because it started to pour. We finished our picnic in the kitchen.

"Do you see the difference? I didn't talk *about* my story. I said the story. I said the actual words I would write. That's important."

Remind children how to listen by demonstrating both how to listen and how *not* to listen

"My second tip is for when you listen. I'm going to show you what not to

Notice that I begin this minilesson as I begin so many minilessons: I name what we've been working on and then tell children what I hope to teach them today. By the end of the connection, students should know what my teaching point will be, and they should sense how today's lesson will fit into the larger context of what I've been teaching them.

In this minilesson, I name what students have been doing a lot that I find problematic. They're often summarizing their stories for their partners rather than using a storyteller's voice to tell the actual story. It helps to act out what students do that is problematic . . . and to act out what I wish they'd do instead.

do. Felecia, will you start to tell me your guinea pig story, and I'm going to show everyone what it looks like when a partner doesn't listen!"

Felecia told about her guinea pig getting fat and hopefully pregnant but it turned out she wasn't a *she* but a *he* and was not having babies. I meanwhile turned my back to Felecia, looked at the ceiling, leaned back in my chair, and picked at my hair.

"Now let me show you what a great listener usually looks like, and then I'm going to ask you to tell your partner the difference. Felecia, would you start the story over?"

Felecia again told her story, and this time I listened leaning toward Felecia, my eyes planted on her, nodding sometimes and smiling at the funny parts.

Active Engagement

Tell the children to turn and talk to their partners about the jobs of storyteller and listeners.

"So talk to your partner about what you've learned about the storyteller's job and the listener's job—about Felecia's job and my job."

Link

Invite the children to plan out stories.

"It's time to resume your writing. I know some of you are in the middle of stories and some are starting new ones. If you are starting a new story, please plan it out with your partner. I'm going to admire ways partners *talk* and *listen* with each other today."

MID-WORKSHOP TEACHING POINT

Point out partners telling stories and listening well.

"Guys, I want all of you to freeze for a moment. Chloe and Sam are being stupendous partners! Will you watch and listen in on what they're doing?" All eyes turned to Chloe and Sam as they talked over Chloe's story.

"Would you be sure your partnership work goes just as well?"

This is a double-decker minilesson. Sometimes it will make sense to tuck a second teaching point into a minilesson, but it's important to be aware that you've done so and to watch for whether children end up not holding onto either of the lessons you hope to teach.

Notice that minilessons do not usually end by the teacher saying, "So, do this today." Instead, minilessons are more apt to end by the teacher saying, "Add this to your repertoire. Use this lesson when you need it as a writer."

TIME TO CONFER

Pause and think about what you are doing to support your English language learners. Even if you feel awkward and are uncertain quite what to say that might make sense, you need to interact with these children more, not less, than you interact with other children. Use "What's the Story in This Picture?" and "Can You Tell a Story and Show it on the Paper?" from the *Conferring with Primary Writers* book as a guide, but let the children guide you, too. Pay close attention to whatever the child has said or done. If these children are literate in their first languages, you may want to encourage some of them to write in their first language and then label their pictures in English. If possible, partner children with each other so they receive more conversational input. When children tell you their stories, try to listen in order to understand, and don't act as if you understand if in fact you are confused. Your effort to make sense of their stories will be crucial. Above all, you need to interact with your English language learners in ways that make them more engaged, more active, and more apt to use language to make meaning.

Be sure that you are conferring with your strong writers as well as with children who need basic support. Use "Can You Recreate That Part . . . ?" and "What Is the Most Important Part . . . ?" from the *Conferring with Primary Writers* book as a guide if you are supporting especially strong writers.

These conferences in *The Conferring Handbook* may be especially helpful today:

▶ *"Will You Touch Each Page and Say What You'll Write?"*

▶ *"Let Me Help You Put Some Words Down"*

▶ *"As a Reader, I'd Love to Hear More About That"*

Also, if you have *Conferring with Primary Writers*, you may want to refer to the following conferences:

▶ "What's the Story in This Picture?"

▶ "Can You Tell a Story and Show It on the Paper?"

▶ "Can You Recreate That Part in a Way That Shows Me Exactly What Happened?"

▶ "What Is the Most Important Part of Your Story?"

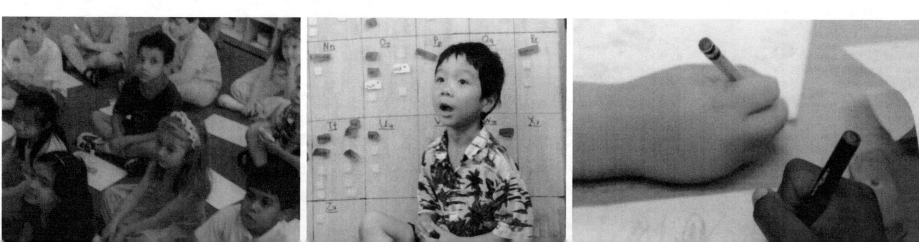

Ask partners to share their stories and revisit their plans to see if anything is missing.

"Many of you told your stories to your partners earlier today. Would you return to your partners now and read your stories? Partners, listen. Did the writers include everything? Did they leave anything out? Give each other tips on how to make these into the *best stories* in the world."

As children read to each other, Abby circled among them noting ways partners supported each other. "I love the way you are looking at your partner while he tells his story," she said. "Ask your partner to say the words she's going to write. Ask her, 'How will you start your story? What will you say exactly?'" Abby reminded partners that it helps if the storyteller either touches the pages of his or her booklet or "tells the story across his fingers."

- You could read aloud about an author who is known for telling stories and for deciding to write the oral stories into books. Patricia Polacco, Tomie dePaola, and Robert Munsch definitely have done this, but there are lots more.
- Listen together to a tape of a storyteller and suggest children get some tips that'll make their storytelling even better. The specific tips will probably not end up being as important as the fact that you spotlight the fact that authors often tell their stories very, very well.
- Children will invariably say more than they write. Partners can listen to a story and then later hear how the writer recorded the story and find a page that isn't as good as the oral version of that page. The writer and his or her partner could work together to imagine how the one page could be improved. Often revising one page leads to other revisions.
- If you ask children to listen to a storyteller telling his or her story on audiotape, children will notice that the storyteller speaks in the voice of characters. Chances are good that your children won't include direct quotations into their stories. You may want to suggest they revise so as to include the voices of their characters. An easy half-step is to suggest children incorporate speech-balloons into their pictures.

WRITING SOME WORDS IN A SNAP

WORD WALL
WORDS

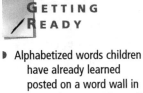

GETTING READY

▶ Alphabetized words children have already learned posted on a word wall in large, clear type where all of the children can see them

▶ Story you used in a previous session, written out part-way on chart paper; stop right before a bunch of high-frequency words need to be written

▶ Marker

▶ White boards and markers for the children

◉ See CD-ROM for resources

THE RESEARCHER SANDRA WILDE HAS FOUND *that half the words children write are the same thirty-six words. How helpful it is, then, if children can write these words effortlessly! This allows children to focus on their content, word choice, audience, purpose, and on the words they don't know with automaticity. Very young writers will not have had enough experience yet with high-frequency words to be able to use a great many with automaticity, but it's important to teach them early on that it's helpful for a writer to "just know" some words, and to be able to spell them in a snap.*

In this session, you'll show children that there are words they "just know" and can spell easily and that the word wall contains other words that they'll "just know" very soon.

The Minilesson

Connection

Remind children of a story you started to write together awhile back. Tell them you want to teach them a strategy that will make writing a long story like that a little easier.

"Writers, yesterday you helped me plan how I'd write the story of the picnic with my cousin. Remember we decided to write, 'Nan and I started to eat sandwiches in the garden. We were laughing . . .' and it kept going. It was a lo-o-o-ng story, with all those details! I started writing it last night but I didn't finish it. I figured we could write some together. I want to teach you a trick for how to make writing go faster."

Teaching

Tell the children that there are some words they will just know and write quickly, and some words they can write after a quick check of the word wall.

"There are some words you guys, as readers, just know." I snapped my fingers to suggest that it's a snap to read these words. "Well, when we write, we also need a handful of words we just know in a snap." I snapped. "That makes writing go faster. So if you are writing a story and you want to write *Mom*, you say, '*Mom*! I know Mom: *M-o-m*!' And you write M-o-m. I put words up here on our word wall that are words I think you know in a snap, or *almost* know in a snap. If there's a word you are writing in your story that is on the word wall, but you can't spell it, you can just look for it there. Then you can say the letters to remind yourself. Once it is in your brain, write it down on your page—snap, snap, snap!"

"Today, we need to add on to our story. I already wrote this."

We were laughing and talking. Then a raindrop landed on my hand. We didn't want

It helps to return to a single story across a sequence of days, as I do in this minilesson. It makes sense for one minilesson to focus on macro-issues such as how to plan a text, and for the next minilesson to zoom in on a micro-issue such as today's emphases on the fact that writers build up and rely upon a knowledge of high-frequency words.

The truth is that it is crucial for children's reading as well as for their writing that they develop a repertoire of words they know with automaticity. The easiest words will be nouns and pronouns such as Mom *and* me. *These words, and others that are a bit harder, can be displayed under their first letter on an alphabetically organized word wall. Teach children that if they want to write a word they almost know my heart and it's on the word wall, they should look at the word, fix it into their mind, then try to write it from memory. That way children are constantly growing their repertoire of known words.*

"Now we need to write this."

to go in, but we did

"Would you get out your wipe boards so we can write more of our story? Maybe some of the words will be ones you know in a snap. Our next word is *to*. Some of you know *to* in a snap? If you don't know it, say *to* and listen for the first sound. Then find it on the word wall under that letter." I enacted this. "So, I either just know *to*, or I look up here and fix the spelling into my brain."

"Okay, write *to*. Let me see. Great. Check it on the word wall." They did. "Spell it (*t-o*)."

Active Engagement

Repeat the process of writing a sight word, referencing the word wall.

"Let's try it again. We've written 'We didn't want to. . . .' Now we need to write *go*. Write it like a snap and move on to the next word, *in*, write it like a snap, or use the word wall to help you. Good work."

I read what most children had written, voiced the next word, *but*, and said, "Keep going with the next word on your wipe boards." They continued, writing *but*.

If the children need it, offer more practice. Tell a story about a child wanting to write a word, ask children to use their knowledge of the word wall to help the child.

"Let's practice one last time. Wipe boards ready? Let's say Amos wanted to write 'I ate ice cream.' *I*, write *I*."

"Let's say Danielle wanted to write 'I love reading.' Write *love*. And check the board if you need to, fixing the letters in your brain so you'll remember them next time."

"Let's say Paul wanted to say, 'My Dad and I rode bikes.' *Dad*, write *Dad*."

When you have tools in your classroom like a word wall, it is important to actually teach children how to use that tool. Act out how you go about finding a word on the word wall. Show children that if you want to write school *and it is on the word wall, you don't copy the word letter-for-letter. Instead, you look at it, noticing whatever stands out. School sounds like it should contain a* k *but instead it begins with* sch. *School contains two* o's. *Once a child has noticed surprising features in a word, the child should be able to write the word without copying . . . and run to check the effort against the listed spelling.*

The words that you have posted on the word wall should be ones that the children use often in their writing, or words that they would like to use.

Link

Remind children that they now know they can write words from memory, or from a combination of memory and the word wall.

"Today, when you write, lots of times you'll come to words you just know. Write these fast. Don't stretch them out—just say, 'I know that word!'" I snapped, "and write it. Or say 'I almost know that word, let me check the word wall' and then write it with a snap!"

"Every day, whenever you write, you'll find words you know like a snap. And as you keep learning, you'll have more and more of these words."

When teaching young children, I find myself inventing a new language. Instead of telling children that they'll come upon high frequency words, I say, "You'll come to words you know in a snap." Instead of saying, "You'll be writing focused personal narratives," I say, "You'll be writing Small Moment stories." I find that I use the same terms over and over, and I use them all year. When I say, "Eyes, please," children know I mean that I want their eyes to be on me or on whomever is speaking. When I say, "Can you tell the story across your fingers," children know what this means.

Of course, the words that the co-authors of this series and I use aren't crucial. You may prefer to use the technical term "high frequency words" or to refer to these as "word wall words." What does matter is that you return to the same terms often so that they convey meaning within the community of your classroom.

Sometimes it is very important for you to be sure that your conferences support your minilesson. Today is one of these days. It won't be in minilessons that children learn to spell a growing number of words with automaticity or to use the words they know to help them write more fluently. These lessons are best taught in conferences.

Sit near children as they write. Ask a child, "What will you write next?" When the child says a sentence think, "Which of these words might be in the child's repertoire of known words?" Then watch the child as he or she writes. If you see the child begin to sound out a word that you suspect the child knows, intervene early on. Say "*Love* . . . you know *love*." See if that nudge, alone, works. If the child guesses, say, "That's a smart guess. Check it with the word wall. What part did you get right?" If a child doesn't know a word that you suspect is within the child's ability as the child approaches the word you say, "*The*. You know *t-h-e*," as a way to show children how helpful it is to merely access the known spelling of these words. If the child spells a word-wall word incorrectly, let the child keep going. When he or she reaches the end of the message, the child can check his or her spellings against those that are posted.

These conferences in *The Conferring Handbook* may be especially helpful today:

▸ *"Will You Touch Each Page and Say What You'll Write?"*
▸ *"Let Me Help You Put Some Words Down"*
▸ *"As a Reader, I'd Love to Hear More About That"*

Also, if you have *Conferring with Primary Writers*, you may want to refer to the conferences in part two.

AFTER-THE-WORKSHOP SHARE

Share the story of one child who used the word wall well today.

"Today I saw Carlina doing something fabulous! I watched her as she was writing and writing and writing, and then I saw her pause for a moment. I could tell that she was thinking about something important. Then she did such a smart thing! She looked over to the word wall and she studied a word up there. Then she wrote the word on her paper, and checked it with the posted word. Carlina, what word did you find on the word wall?"

"I got the word *what*. I knew it started with /wh/ /wh/. So I looked under *w*. It had a *h*! I put it in my mind and I wrote it."

"It was fantastic that Carlina thought to look to the word wall for the spelling of *what*. I also loved that she didn't just copy the word. She learned how to spell it. She put it in her mind. Then she tried writing it without looking! That was a spectacular use of a writing tool!"

Ask the children to practice writing a few more words like a snap—with or without the word wall. Give them several words to write from the wall, one at a time.

"Let's all practice using the word wall with our partners. I'll say a word aloud. If you and your partner can write it like a snap, do that. If you can't write the word, say it with your partner and then tell each other where you'd look on the word wall. Then find it." I said about six words, and they wrote them together.

As usual, it is no accident that Carlina describes her work so clearly. She has had a chance to rehearse what she will say in a conference during the writing time, as I talked with her.

You'll want to do this sort of work at other times in the day as well as now. Children need to be taught to use the tools of a writing workshop. Don't assume anything!

FOCUSING ON THE MOST IMPORTANT PART

GETTING READY

▶ Unfocused story from your life in mind

▶ Focused version of the same story in mind

◉ See CD-ROM for resources

WHEN MANY OF US WERE IN *elementary school, our teachers taught us that the qualities of good writing that mattered most include descriptive language, adjectives, and simile. Most writers, however, tend to worry far more about focus than about descriptive language. Writers know that if our focus is clear, the wonderful words often follow as day follows night.*

This minilesson is designed to remind children to focus their writing. For now, focus *means limiting the size—the scope—of a subject. It refers to the process of zooming in on a smaller subject. Focus allows details to emerge. (Later, the term* focus *can refer to a writer's angle of vision. A writer can write about a tree as a home for animals, as a collage of color, as a shelter from the sun. Either way the subject is the same and it's the angle of vision or the message about the tree that changes. This is a more advanced understanding of focus.)*

In this session, you will demonstrate that writers think "What is the most important part of my story?" and that they make that aspect of their story important by adding details to that part and by cutting away the other parts.

THE MINILESSON

Connection

Tell the children how writers zoom in and focus like photographers.

"Today I am going to teach you that writers are like photographers. Photographers can look out of their cameras and see that whole wall of our classroom with charts and books and plants and the clock and the fish tank and the chairs. Or they can zoom in and see just one thing, like just our fish tank, but now they see all the details in the tank. They even see the blue eyes of our guppy! Writers can also write about the whole wall, the whole world, but usually writers, like photographers, want to zoom close in. I am going to show you how writers, like photographers, zoom in on the most important parts of our stories."

Ford couldn't resist, "Abby, the binoculars I got for my birthday, you put them near your eyes and you see everything close!"

"Ford, that is a smart way of explaining zooming in. When you zoom in, you see things closely."

Teaching

Tell the children to watch you tell your story aloud. Tell a list-like, unfocused story.

"First I am going to think of a big whole thing in my life." Abby paused. "Okay, I am remembering when I went to see my Nana in the hospital. We played cards. Then, I took her outside. We held hands and talked. We ate lunch and then I said good-bye." With her hands, Abby showed that her topic was big, like the whole classroom wall, although actually it was already more focused than the topics children often take on.

Suki called out, "That sounds like *a list* of the day."

Throughout this year-long curriculum, you'll find that your minilessons often rely on metaphor. We'll teach children that writers don't write on big watermelon topics like "recess" but on tiny-seed topics like "When I fell off the monkey bars." Here Abby suggests that writers, like photographers, need to zoom in on the most important part of their subject. Instead of writing about the field, a writer writes about a clump of three daisies. Many children love these metaphors and learn from them, but at first some children will find the metaphor confusing. The answer is not to give up on metaphor, but you may find that some children benefit from small group work designed to help them grasp the meaning and significance of terms and concepts you'll use often. Your English language learners, for example, may need you to show them that you could write about a big topic like the group of children or zoom in and write about one child's foot!

Demonstrate how you will zoom in on the most important part of the unfocused story. Tell them the focused story aloud.

"Yeah, I did just kind of list all the things I did with my Nana. But now what I am going to zoom in." Abby's hands showed that she was going to bring her attention in from a topic the size of a whole wall to a topic that was more like the size of fish tank. "I'll zoom in and write just about *the most important part* of the memory!" She paused. "Oh I know! My Nana and I put our hands up to each other's and noticed that our hands were the same exact size. My story will sound like this:"

> At lunch, my Nana and I held our hands up against each other. My skin wasn't as wrinkly as hers, but our hands were exactly the same size and shape. Then my Nana just took hold of my hand and held it. I squeezed her hand back because I loved being with my Nana that day.

Active Engagement

Ask your children to reread their most recent story, asking, "Is it focused?" After they do this, suggest they tell their partners the most important part of that story.

"Would you all open your folders and recall the story you'll be working on today? Would you reread that story and ask, 'Is this big (like the classroom wall or my whole visit to my Nana) or zoomed-in and small (like the fish tank or my Nana and I comparing hands)?' If it's big, would you tell your partner how you could zoom in, if you decided to do that?"

Abby listened in on some of the partners' conversations. Evan, for example, said, "My most important part is that I saw this mummy at the museum and he was all wrapped up and my sister was so scared but I wasn't scared. I'm bigger."

Link

Remind the students to zoom in on the most important part of the memory when they write today and every day.

Abby signaled for the class to come back together. "When you write today and every day, think about being a photographer and about *zooming in* on the most important part of your memory!" Some children returned to pieces they'd begun earlier, and others chose paper and began new stories.

Notice that at this early level of teaching, we tend to use true stories from our lives rather than children's literature as examples of good writing. We can design our own writing so that it is lean and so that we make the point we want to make in very few words. Sometimes you may have trouble thinking up stories that will work with kids. The secret is to keep your own writer's notebook and to live writerly lives just as you are asking your children to do. Just as photographers see potential pictures everywhere, people who write see potential stories everywhere.

Notice that the minilesson on any one day will not usually be applicable to all children on that day because every child will be at a different place in the writing process.

MID-WORKSHOP TEACHING POINT

Remind children of all they know about writing down sounds they hear in words by telling the class what a few, brave children have been doing.

"Writers, I have been noticing how you have been using more and more words to tell your stories well. Such beautiful words have been coming out! For example, Danya stretched out *sparkling* and Lavelle wrote *hippopotamus*. Wow—what big words! For a minute, before you get back to writing, may we practice our strategy of stretching words out together? Remember, we say the word slowly, write down the sound we hear, reread, say the word, write down the sound, reread. . . ."

Offer practice in getting words on paper by having children join in the spelling venture of one child.

"So Jake was writing about how he went pumpkin picking. *Pumpkin*— what a beautiful word to stretch. On the back of your story paper, would you all help Jake stretch out and record all the sounds you hear in the word *pumpkin*?"

Abby walked around to see the children's work. After a moment or so she signaled to them.

"So writers, let's work on *pumpkin* together." Abby went through the process and ended up writing *PMKN* on the easel. "Wonderful, writers."

If it hasn't taken too long, practice another word with them.

"Let's try Lavelle's word—are you ready? Try writing *hippopotamus*. Before you do, let's clap the parts of that word." Abby and the class did. "Take just the first part and write that." They did. "Fingers under it, let's read what we have so far: *hip*. What's the next part? *po*. Write that and keep going till you've written the whole word."

"As you write today and every day, when you want to spell a word, stretch it out using this strategy. I can't wait to hear and see the beautiful words you write!"

Act as if you know your children share your appreciation for words. Invite them to join you in relishing long words . . . and to approach the challenge of spelling words with energy.

When you teach children to tackle long words, you are teaching them to read as well as to write. If a child has written part of the word and still has more to write, that child needs to do some careful reading in order to determine what has been and needs to be written.

TIME TO CONFER

As on most days, you'll want to begin the workshop by saying, "Get started. I'm just going to research—and admire—the work you're doing." Resist getting sucked into one-to-one conferences right away. You want to be sure children are able to get themselves started without needing you to give them each a personal nudge. Once they are working, you can confer.

Among other things, when you confer today you will want to help children realize that the lessons from any one minilesson pertain to every other day. This means that on any given day, you'll help some children sketch rather than draw their pictures, and you'll help others add details or hear sounds or spell some words or tell stories across their fingers. Meanwhile, in some conferences you'll discover and address issues that haven't been addressed yet in minilessons. If several children seem as if they'd profit from the same instruction, convene a small group and lead a strategy lesson. You could design a strategy lesson to help children zoom in on a focused vignette or to help children hear and record sounds.

These conferences in *The Conferring Handbook* may be especially helpful today:

- ▶ *"Will You Touch Each Page and Say What You'll Write?"*
- ▶ *"Let Me Help You Put Some Words Down"*
- ▶ *"As a Reader, I'd Love to Hear More About That"*

Also, if you have *Conferring with Primary Writers*, you may want to refer to the conferences in part two.

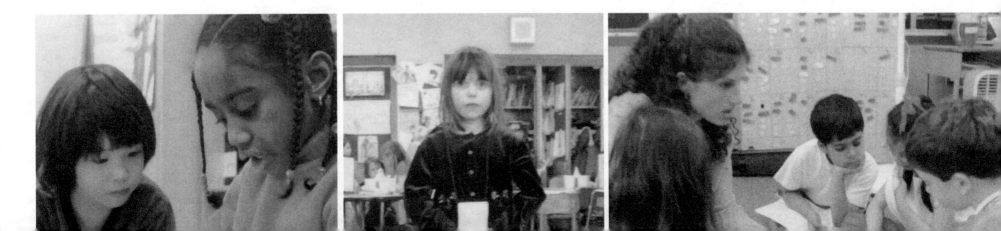

Call the children to the carpet and tell them about how a child zoomed in on the most important part.

"Writers, I have something really special to share with you. Jared was going to write all about how he went to the baseball game with his dad and they got hot dogs and ice cream and then took the subway back to the city and then went to his cousin's house," Abby said this in a drone. "But then Jared stopped and said, 'No, I am going to try and be like Vera Williams and like Audrey and zoom in on the most important part,' and he zoomed in on the part about getting the hot dogs. Listen to his story."

My dad got me a hot dog. I put ketchup all over it. Then I slowly ate it
bite by bite till it was all gone.

"Did you hear that beautiful Small Moment about just the hot dog?"

▶ If you decide to teach another minilesson designed to help children focus their stories, you might tell the story of how Donald Crews wrote one book, *Bigmama's,* about his whole summer vacation. Then he wrote *Shortcut* about one incident that occurred one evening during vacation.

▶ You may want to create a minilesson around the idea that a writer often tells a story across his or her fingers; the writer sometimes takes just one part—one finger—of the original tale and makes this into a whole story.

▶ Sometimes children worry that if they focus on one brief part of their story, their tale will be very short. Help them understand that they could write a one-sentence story about you putting on your coat ("Our teacher put on her coat."), or they could tell this bit-by-bit so that it is a very long story ("First our teacher held up her coat. She reached one arm into. . . .").

When you bring your children's work home and look over what they've done, you'll probably find yourself making two categories: okay and not-okay work. And then, if you are anything like Abby and me, your tendency will be to focus on the work that worries you. You are wise to pay special attention to these children, and especially wise if you become accustomed to looking for the small steps ahead that these writers are making. Don't allow yourself to feel overwhelmed over the fact that you don't see progress, because more than anything, these children need to feel themselves getting stronger and to take pleasure and gain confidence in the fact that, step by step, they are learning to write. The small steps ahead *should* be there, and you need to see them and to exalt in them. Your excitement will give your children a precious energy source.

Meanwhile, don't overlook the writing of others who are doing fairly well. It's important to also look with great care at the charming, sequential little stories that most of your students are writing. What is it that these children seem able to do? You'll want to be able to put into words what it is that works in your children's writing. You'll want to grow accustomed to looking at good work and asking, "What has this writer done in this piece that he or she will want to do again in other pieces? What has this writer done that others might emulate?"

You'll also want to look at your very most successful writers' texts to see what these writers haven't quite achieved. Lucille Clifton, the great poet, once said, "We cannot create what we cannot imagine." You can't help your children's writing become stronger unless you can imagine next steps for them.

For Abby and me, it was easy to envision the horizon for her kindergarteners because we met once a week with a study group of K–1 teachers, and each week Pat Bleichman, Marjorie Martinelli, Carrie

Strauss, and others came laden down with examples of what their first graders produced in a parallel unit of study.

Sometimes Abby and I would get hold of even the very typical, everyday pieces from their classrooms, and we'd ask, "What are these first graders doing that our kindergarteners aren't yet doing? Might we teach our little ones to work in similar ways?"

As Eric's and Pippa's books suggest (they were both written in early October), one of the big differences between kindergarten and first grade was the sentence complexity. [*Fig. XI-1* and *XI-2*]

Then, too, the first graders tended to have a bit of fun with language, often adding dialogue or sound effects or words that created a mood. These latter observations led Abby and me to imagine new frontiers for her youngsters. We knew that the final round of minilessons in this unit would probably address her most adventurous writers (those who need a lot of repetition might not reach these heights), but we were glad to bring new frontiers to her youngsters.

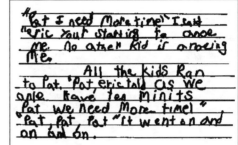

I was so mad. I stomped my foot.
Steam was coming out of my eyes.
"I want more time to plant," in my head I was saying.
"I need more time," it went on and on.

"Pat, I need more time," I said.
"Eric, you're starting to annoy me. No other kid is annoying me."
All the kids ran to Pat. "Pat, Eric told us we only have ten minutes. Pat, we need more time!"
"Pat, Pat, Pat," it went on and on and on.

Fig. XI-1   Eric

When My Zipper Got Stuck
I put my hand on my zipper. I pulled and pulled and nothing happened. The zipper didn't move. Everybody tried to unzip it but it wouldn't move.

There was one person to try. The nurse. The nurse put her hand on my zipper. She pulled up and down, up and down, up and down. The she pulled all the way down.

Fig. XI-2   Pippa

91

REVEALING INTERNAL STORIES

GETTING READY

▸ Writing that depicts what happened and the narrator's response to what happened (it's best if the model is written by a child of the same or close age as your children, but it need not be from a student in your present class)

● See CD-ROM for resources

ONCE YOUR CHILDREN BECOME ACCUSTOMED *to zooming in and writing chronological retellings of small vignettes and once they are recording the major sounds they hear in words and using high frequency words, you will probably want to help them write their stories in ways that are more and more effective. One important way to improve children's stories is for children to alternate between describing actions—writing the external story—and revealing thoughts and feelings—writing the accompanying internal story. Often when any of us write personal narratives, our first tendency is to simply retell the timeline of events. Maxine Kumin, a poet, once said that when she reread what she'd written in a journal she realized, "I am too busy living the life of wife, mother and child to unfold. It's all in the pleats." Young children may not be too busy living the life of wife or mother, but their narratives, like Maxine Kumin's, often leave a great deal in the pleats. In this minilesson, you will help children unfold the pleats and bring out their internal stories. You will teach them to write not only the action but also the reaction. You'll do this by using an example. After naming and discussing what the one child has done in his writing, you'll ask all your children to try to do similar work as they work with a partner to revise a story you give them.*

In this session, you will help children unfold the pleats and reveal the internal stories (the reactions, thoughts, observations, feelings) in their pieces.

THE MINILESSON

Connection

Tell children that today you will teach a new strategy for stretching out a Small Moment. The strategy involves writing not only the external but also the internal events.

"Writers, we have been talking about taking Small Moments from our lives and stretching them out so we can 'tell them long.' We know that Vera does this in her writing and now we are the kind of writers who do this, too."

"Well, today I want to tell you about a strategy you can use to say more about your Small Moment. I'm going to show you that you can write what happened," my gesture indicated that this is, on the one hand, one option, "and then you can show your response to what happened, your feelings or thoughts about what happened." My gesture suggested this is an alternate way to write.

Teaching

Read an exemplar piece of writing that retells not only what happened but also the writer's response to what happened.

"Writers, I am going to read you a piece that Tatyana wrote. Tatyana was in Abby's class last year and now she is in first grade. I want you to be researchers and really listen closely to how Tatyana wrote this Small Moment of laying down on her mother's lap. She told what happened, and then she told what she thought and felt about what happened." I read the piece aloud, slowing down and pausing briefly to emphasize what I wanted the children to notice. [*Fig. XII-1*]

In this minilesson, I'm not extending the work we've been doing lately, and so, instead of retelling the specifics of yesterday's minilesson, I recall the general mission of this unit of study.

The Hug and Kiss
Before bed my mom gave me a hug and a kiss. I was sitting on her lap and I was lying on her shoulders. I felt so comfy.

Fig. XII-1   Tatyana

"What'd you notice?"

Ford put his thumb up for me to call on him, trying to sit like a pretzel despite his huge cowboy boots. "Tatyana told us she was cozy lying on her mom."

"Wow. Ford, I noticed that, too! She wrote what she did," I gestured with the right hand, "how she sat on her mom's lap and lay on her shoulders—but she also write how she felt," I gestured with the other hand, "and she wrote that in a very honest way. She wrote the outside story of what she did and the inside story of how she felt!" I gestured with both hands in sequence as I said this.

Active Engagement

Ask the class to turn and talk to their partners about telling the inside and the outside story.

"Researchers, turn and talk to your partner about how Tatyana wrote what happened and what she felt about what happened."

Clarissa and Raphael turned to each other and sat knee to knee. Clarissa said, "I like my mom too. She is so, so, so, so sweet."

"Yeah, I like cuddling with my mommy," Raphael added, as he put his index finger to his temple as if he were thinking very intensely.

At Abby's school, P.S. 116, all the teachers across all the grades encourage children to do "The Magic Five," a phrase that encapsulates the five expectations of acting like a good listener. Children know they are to follow these guidelines:

- *Sit like a pretzel*
- *Eyes on the person who is talking (of course, this is often a classmate)*
- *Ears listening*
- *Hands in laps*
- *Mouths quiet when someone else is speaking*

Gestures are helpful when teaching very young children. When I suggest that it is important to tell the external story, I gesture with one hand, and then I gesture to show that, on the other hand, it is also important to tell the internal story. I'll use these gestures again later in the minilesson.

Remind everyone of an event in the classroom each is sure to remember. Ask the children to tell the inside story and the outside story of that event to their partner.

"Remember Miss Crystal's party? Let's work together to tell the outside *and* the inside story. Let's retell the story of that party using two hands." Holding up one hand, "On the one hand, tell the actual things that happened when Miss Crystal came in the room and we yelled, 'Surprise!'" They told the story. I held up the other hand, "On the other hand, tell what you thought or felt when Miss Crystal came in and we yelled, 'Surprise!'" Again the room erupted into talk.

Repeat for the class an outside and inside story that you overheard partners talking about.

Reiterating, I held up the first hand and said, "First what happened on the outside," and then I held up the other hand, "Then what happened on the inside." Then I said, "I heard George say the outside story first. 'We hid in the coat closet and waited until Miss Crystal came in. Then we jumped out and said, "Surprise!"' Then George said what he was thinking and feeling, the inside story. He said, 'Miss Crystal almost cried, and I did too because I don't want her to leave.'"

Link

Encourage and invite the students to try this strategy in their own writing.

"When you write today and from now on, try to remember that on the one hand, you can tell what happened. But then, on the other hand, you can tell what you thought and felt. Then you can go back to what happened. Today, if you write not just the outside story but also the inside story, come and get me so I can admire your work."

The challenge when one is writing is to shift from retelling the chronological sequence of events to elaborating upon one event by describing how you felt or what you thought at any one time. In this active involvement, I make the task much easier for children because I set them up to do just the one—retelling the events—or just the other—describing their thoughts and feelings. During conferences, I'll have to help children make the transition between the one and the other as they write.

Notice that the example is lean, brief. Avoid using lush, long stories to make your points because often the point gets lost in the detail.

I gesture to match my words.

TIME TO CONFER

Today's minilesson was meant to stretch your writers and to give them a horizon to work towards. You may want to confer or to lead a strategy lesson designed to help writers incorporate the lesson from today into their writing. You might want to rely on a children's book to help you in your conferences. Find a book your children know and love. *Salt Hands* by Jane Chelsea Aragon works well. The author describes the tiniest details of seeing a deer on the lawn outside her house and going out to feed the deer from her salt hands. Each tiny step forward in action also chronicles what the narrator thought, noticed, felt, remembers. See the conference cited at right.

Meanwhile, this unit of study is rounding its final bend and so you'll want to use the conferring checklist to remind you of essential goals you want to help every child reach. Your conferences today will resemble those that will be mainstays of your Revision unit of study and so you may want to peek ahead and study those.

These conferences in *The Conferring Handbook* may be especially helpful today:

- ▶ *"I See You're Adding an Exclamation Mark to Your Story Like Mem Fox Does"*
- ▶ *Conferences in part four*

Also, if you have *Conferring with Primary Writers*, you may want to refer to the conferences in part two and in part four.

Admire the way children write the outside and the inside story and share examples.

"Writers, it was amazing to see how your pieces changed today when you began to write not only what you did but also what you thought and felt. You are writing not just the outside story but also the inside story."

"Heather could have written her story like this."

> Two years ago my brother graduated from college. All the graduators walked down the aisle. I saw my brother. More people came. Then we went home.

"Let me reread what Heather wrote and let's notice if she's telling what happened on the outside or what she thought and felt and noticed and wished for on the inside." [*Fig. XII-3*]

> Two years ago my brother graduated from college. All the graduators walked down the aisle. I saw my brother. I was happy he saw me. Inside I felt good. More and more people came.

Ask children to reread their work with partners to see if they can see past the outside story to the inside story.

"Would you all reread what you wrote today and if you find a place in your story where you wrote the inside story like Heather did, put one finger on that part of your text and give me a thumbs up." They reread. Half put thumbs up. "Great!"

Fig. XII-3   Heather

Two years ago my brother graduated from college. All the graduators walked down the aisle. I saw my brother. I was happy he saw me. Inside I felt good. More and more people came.

▶ Tell the class the story of a child who wrote his Small Moment story in a way that recorded not only the external but also the internal story. Before reading the text, explain how the author wrote like Tatyana. "Wow. Ethan was like Tatyana. He wrote about his baseball game. Listen to how he told not only what he did, the outside story, but also what he was thinking, the inside story."

▶ Give a second example, again highlighting the fact that the author included the internal and the external story. This time, emphasize that the child could have just described the sequence of events. "Glenn could have written, 'At my birthday party, I blew out the candles and everyone sang happy birthday to me,' but instead he wrote, 'At my birthday party, I got to blow out my candles. The day reminded me of a holiday. Everyone sang happy birthday to me and I didn't know whether to sit there or to sing too. So I sang to myself. It was embarrassing but nice.'"

▶ Invite your class to be researchers and to listen as you read pieces aloud. Do they contain the external and the internal story? You could ask the class to show with gestures when, on the one hand, the external story is recorded and when, on the other hand, the internal story is told.

▶ Give the class a list of phrases that can help them get started writing the internal story. Then ask partners to practice using these phrases to bring out the internal story into a bit of shared writing: "We were about to go out to recess. We opened the door to run out and saw it was raining." "I thought," "I wondered," "I noticed," "I wished," "I worked to say," "I remembered," "I felt."

WRITING CLOSE-IN STORY ENDINGS

GETTING READY

- A shared experience story that ends in a way that resembles children's less-than-great endings
- Beginning of another shared experience story written out on large chart paper booklet, with a close-in ending or two in mind
- Optional: a story of a shared experience that has a weak ending written on chart paper
- Marker
- See CD-ROM for resources

IN THIS UNIT, YOU WANT CHILDREN *to take on the rhythms and language of story, and the endings are crucial to that. Endings are also crucial because they are the last words a reader reads, and therefore they leave a lasting impression. One writer said that poems and stories are like love affairs—we can forgive anything if they have a good ending. (You wouldn't tell this to the children!)*

Many of your children probably end their pieces "and then I went home," or "I went to bed." In this minilesson, you'll teach children some guidelines for writing effective endings, suggesting that often it helps to stay closer to the heart of the story rather than leaping away to say, "And then I went home." You'll demonstrate how you find an ending to one story, and then you'll help your children develop an ending to a story.

In this session, you will teach children some guidelines for writing effective story endings, suggesting that it often helps to stay closer to the heart of the story rather than writing away from it.

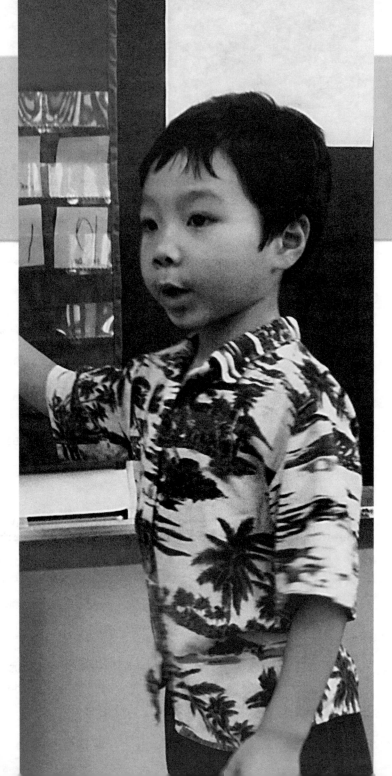

Connection

Compliment the children on their Small Moment stories and tell them sometimes their story endings need work. Say, "Often your stories tend to end like this . . ." and give examples.

"I've loved reading your stories, especially now that they stretch the moments out—except guys, I have to tell you one thing. Sometimes your stories are so great," I held my hand up high as if the stories are so tall, "and your endings are a letdown." I brought my hands low. "Your stories go like this:"

Yesterday a lady came to our class to teach us about snakes. She took one from the crate. It wrapped around her arm. We each touched it.

Then my intonation changed to suggest that, oh dear, everything falls apart.

Then we went home.

"What a letdown! Today we'll learn how to write endings that are as wonderful as your stories."

Teaching

Tell children how you see them ending stories. If they jump far away from the Small Moment, suggest they find endings within their moments.

"What you do now is that you usually write endings that jump away from the Small Moment. So you tell the story about that lady bringing the snake to our room and end it with, 'Then we had lunch' or 'Then we went home.' Do you see how you are jumping away from the Small Moment and going to a whole different time?"

"It doesn't have to go that way. You will usually get a better ending if you stay *close-in to the moment*. Let's try that together. I'll read the story again and will you think how you could end it, still staying *close-in* to the snake lady's visit?"

You may squirm at the bluntness of my opening words, but children giggle, enjoying my lighthearted complaining and recognizing that indeed their books do end, "And then I went home" or "And then I went to bed." You could even afford to play this up a bit more, perhaps picking up a few dearly loved examples of children's literature saying, "What if Maurice Sendak wrote this . . ." and then reading the second-to-last page, adding in a "blah" voice "and then I went home."

This minilesson is a rich and complex one so use your hands and your voice to bring home your meaning. Your voice should jump away from the Small Moment when you describe how their endings often go.

Ask the class to join you in writing a new ending for the story you cited earlier. Think aloud to get them started searching for an ending within the moment. Offer several possible endings and how you got to them.

> Yesterday a lady came to out class to teach us about snakes. She took one snake from the crate. It coiled around her arm. We each touched it.

"Hmmm . . . One way to end a story is to remember back to the very next thing that happened. I'm trying to remember . . . I think she said, 'Isn't he handsome?' and put him away. Couldn't that be an ending?"

> It coiled around her arm. We each touched it. "Isn't he handsome?" she said and put him away.

"Another way to end the story while staying in the moment is to say what you thought or felt (the inside story) during that moment. What did you think or feel when she said, 'Isn't he handsome?'"

> Lucas said, "I felt nervous. I wanted to say, 'No,' but I said, 'I guess.'" "So couldn't *that* be our ending?" The story would go like this:"

> It coiled around her arm. We each touched it. "Isn't she handsome?" she said and put him away. I felt nervous. I wanted to say, "No," but I said, "I guess."

"Do you see how one way to write story endings is to end the story while staying in the moment? Another way is to tell what you thought or felt in the moment—to tell a little of the inside story like you learned the other day."

Notice that I didn't call on children to elicit their suggestions. I want them to generate possible endings in their mind, but for now I think they need more demonstrations of what I mean, and the most efficient way to provide these is by writing publicly. If I solicited children's input right now, I suspect it would take us off course.

I could safely elicit input to this question without worrying that the child's response would take us off track.

Notice how I not only tell the children the ending possibilities, but I also tell them ways to get to a close-in ending: They can say what happens next, or they can say how they felt. Of course, there are other ways to end stories too—the key thing here is not only to offer good endings, but to teach children how to get there.

The next section is optional. The existing minilesson could be tweaked to include more active involvement and it could end here rather than including the next episode.

Active Engagement

Tell the class that you need help to write an ending to a story based on a shared experience.

"I have been working again on that story about our surprise party for Miss Crystal. I need you to listen to the story and to work with your partner to see if you could improve my ending."

Read the piece aloud off of a large chart paper booklet.

Miss Crystal was out of the room. We all hid in the coat closet. It was so quiet but everyone kept giggling. We heard a knock at the door. Miss Crystal came in and we yelled, "Surprise!" Then we went home.

Tell the students to turn to their writing partners and talk about whether the story has a good ending. Could they improve on it?

All the children turned to talk to their partner.

Kenar said to Alexa: "She says she goes home. She should tell how we hugged Miss Crystal."

Signal for the class to come back together and ask a child how he would end the story.

"Let's come back together. Kenar, I heard you tell Alexa some good ideas. Could you repeat them for the class?" He did.

Reread the piece, but this time add the ending a student suggested.

"Now listen to how wonderful the story sounds with an ending that's close to the moment." I retold the story, this time adding Kenar's ending.

Miss Crystal was out of the room. We all hid in the coat closet. It was so quiet but everyone kept giggling. We heard a knock at the door. Miss Crystal came in and we yelled, "Surprise!" Then we hugged each other.

Link

Invite and encourage the children to try and think about writing good endings to their stories.

"So when you write today, and every day, if it's time to end your story, pause and ask, 'How can I write a good ending?' And from now on, let's say it's not allowed to end your piece with 'and then I went home' or 'and then I went to sleep.'"

This story was part of an earlier minilesson. As often as possible, let a single story thread through your minilessons.

Of course, you will have deliberately written this story so that it is a Small Moment just like the children have been writing, and so its ending begs for help.

I deliberately set the children up so they have no excuse but to do this and do it well. The problem with this ending isn't a subtle one. It's fairly clear that children will be able to supply a next step in the narrative that will work well.

Grown-up writers would never say, "It's not allowed to . . ." but remember, these are kindergartners and they love inventing the rules!

TIME TO CONFER

Today's minilesson, like the earlier one on the importance of telling the internal as well as the external story, can add tremendous flair to your children's stories. You'll find it rewarding to help children write effective endings—and their stories will become dramatically better as a result. To help children create endings that rise to the occasion of being endings, read children their own writing as if it's the greatest literature in the world, leaving a blank space for an ending. Often, if you read a text with proper resonance, the child can pull a beautiful ending out of the air.

If children can't do this, you may want to demonstrate in your conferences to show children how you generate worthy endings. "Let me show you how I come up with endings," you could say. You could then show children how you reread the text to get a running start on the end, then try out one possible ending (produce a bad one!), weighing whether you like it. Show them that if you don't like it, you repeat this, again generating a possible ending. After you demonstrate doing this, you should be able to say, "So you try it," and get them doing the same thing.

These conferences in *The Conferring Handbook* may be especially helpful today:

▶ *"This Part Is Confusing to Me"*
▶ *"Can You Reenact That Part in a Way That Shows Me How You Felt?"*

Also, if you have *Conferring with Primary Writers*, you may want to refer to the conferences in part two.

Read some pieces, emphasizing how the writers ended the stories. Read the endings slowly and dramatically to show how the endings bring the story towards its conclusion.

"The other day, we heard Heather's story about her brother's graduation. She added an ending, and then decided, 'No, no, I don't like the ending.' Let me read you the story with the ending she didn't like."

> Two years ago my brother graduated from college. All the graduators walked down the aisle. I saw my brother. I was happy he saw me. Inside I felt good. More and more people came. After that we met my brother. Everyone gave him a hug. Then we went on a tour. It was interesting. Then we got a sample of ice cream. It was delicious. "Can I have more?" "We have to go."

"Tell your partner why you think Heather decided that her ending doesn't work." They talked.

"It jumped away, didn't it? So Heather decided to change it, and this time to stay close to the moment." [*Fig. XIII-1*]

> Two years ago my brother graduated from college. All the graduators walked down the aisle. I saw my brother. I was happy he saw me. Inside I felt good. More and more people came. After we met, my brother gave me a hug. I said, "Congratulations, Ben."

"Would you guys reread your endings and see if you think your ending is great or so-so or sort of terrible.'" They did. "How many of you decided your ending was 'sort of terrible'? Good for you to see that! I'm exactly the same as you. When I reread my writing, I often say, 'Oh, no! I could do so much better!'"

"Smart work. Will you guys revise tomorrow? Here's a sticky note. Put it where you have work you know you need to do."

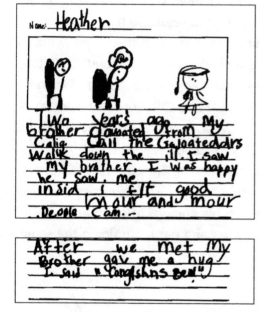

Fig. XIII-1   Heather

Notice that I celebrate when children raise their hands to say their endings are "sort of terrible." I do want children to know that it's a great thing to be critical of one's own writing, and that I, too, often feel this way.

Today's minilesson addressed a very complex concept and your children's understanding of story ending will develop in the fullness of time, with lots of exposure to wonderful stories and lots of discussion about writers' choices. You could certainly teach another minilesson now or during later units of study designed to help writers think carefully about the way they end their stories.

- Celebrate a child's story ending. For example, Sophie, in Abby's class, ended a story about wanting to leave a birthday party with the ending, "I said, 'Daddy, when are we leaving?' and he finally said, 'Right now.'"

- Read a picture book and tell children the author probably tried ten different endings before he or she wrote this one. Then say, "If she'd have ended it like this," and give an example. "What if the ending had gone like this?" you could ask, and give another example.

- You could help children begin to realize that there are a few predictable ways that writers often end their stories. For example, many writers end a story by referring back to the lead. Many authors end a story by having one character speak, saying words that somehow sum up the whole story. Sometimes writers use the onset of evening to help them put a story to bed.

REVISING AND EDITING WITH PARTNERS

GETTING READY

- Each student will have already chosen the piece he or she wants to publish
- Chart from the end of the last unit: "How to Fix Up a Piece"
- Simple story written on chart paper to edit together
- Copy of the same story written on chart paper for each partnership
- Editing marker for each partnership
- See CD-ROM for resources

OFTEN, WHEN TEACHING UPPER-GRADE STUDENTS *or teachers, my colleagues and I say, "Would you think about one time in your life when writing really worked for you?" Almost without fail, every single person will respond by telling the story of a time when he or she was published. "I still remember when the teacher read my story aloud," a child will say, and then add wistfully, "I was an author back then."*

Nothing does more than publication to make us feel like we are really truly authors. Therefore it is crucial to end each unit of study with an author celebration. These needn't be lavish affairs, although even a little pomp and circumstance goes a long way.

You'll want to teach children that writers select their best work for publication day, and they revisit their work thinking, "How can I fix this up so it's my very best?" For now, the most important thing is that writers make the gesture to revise their work. Later we'll teach children a host of strategies for making substantial revisions.

Last month, children reread their writing asking, "Does this make sense?" and "How can I fix it? What can I add?" These questions will continue to guide this month's revisions. This time, however, you may also want to spotlight the way partners help each other to revise writing.

This session will teach children some strategies for making substantial revisions to their pieces, and you'll help writers support their partner's revisions.

THE MINILESSON

Connection

Tell students that it's time to choose work to fix up and fancy up for publication. Tell them that you'll teach them how to use partners as editors during revision.

"Writers, this is an important day. You need to choose the piece that you will publish. I know you remember that we need to fix our writing up just like people fix themselves up for a graduation or a wedding. Today what I want to teach you is that it's really great to have your partner's help when it comes time to fix up your writing."

Teaching

Tell children that editors are writing partners.

"We have already talked about some ways to fix up a piece of our own writing. One thing that we haven't talked about very much is how to fix up another person's writing. This is an important thing to know! All writers in the world have partners to work with, people called *editors*. The job of this partner, our editor, is to go through the piece with us before it is published and find ways to help us fix it up."

> ### HOW TO FIX UP A PIECE
>
> A writer and an editor read it over really carefully.
>
> We ask, "Does this make sense? How can we fix it? What can we add?"
>
> Then we fancy up our pieces.

I'm deliberately comparing the author's celebration to very big events—graduations and weddings. I want to create a drum roll around the upcoming celebration.

The opportunity to publish can make youngsters feel like "real writers," and I want to do everything possible to build on that feeling. I describe the role of editors, then, because it is quite true that writers need the companionship and advice of a good editor, but also because I'm hoping to use the upcoming celebration to help children feel like real writers.

Ask all the students to be your editors, listening to your draft.

"Now, you are all going to be my partners, my editors. I am going to reread my story to you and I want you to listen, like an editor would, to check to see if the piece makes sense."

> Today at reces
> it started rain
> We went inside.

"Does it make sense?"

"Yesss," the children chorused.

Suggest that editors also ask, "Could we add on to this?" and make suggestions

"The next thing that an editor needs to do is to read the piece again and help the writer think about things that could be added. Again, I want you all to be my editors. Let's read the story again and this time, help me think about what we could add."

> Today at reces
> it started rain
> We went inside.

An enthusiastic murmur spread across the rug as children thought of details to add.

"You could tell that we played dominoes."

"And that the fourth graders played with us."

"Wow. You guys have given me such great ideas! It is really helpful to have more than just one person look at my piece. When Kevin suggested that I add about playing dominoes, I hadn't even thought about putting that in!"

"So editors have lots of different jobs." Abby referred to the chart. "They can help you see if your piece makes sense and they can help you add details and they can help with spelling, too. Would you read this and ask, 'Does that look right?' Check that every word seems to be spelled right." Soon the children were suggesting ways to spell recess.

Notice that my draft doesn't go on and on—nor does it represent the best writing I could possibly do. My goal is to be as brief as possible while still making the point I want to make.

Obviously, there are lots of nice things that could be added onto this piece. The goal isn't to create a perfect piece of writing. Instead, the goal is to demonstrate that editors help us a variety of ways. The point is best made if this minilesson moves along briskly.

Notice that Abby is glowing about how helpful it can be to get input. She also reminds children of the ways they, as editors, have helped her. It is important to help children regard suggestions as gifts.

Active Engagement

Ask children to try editing another piece on their own.

"Now, I'm going to read you another piece of writing that I'd like help with."

> Yesterday, I went to visit my grandma.
> She mad a cak for me.
> It so good.

"I'm going to give you and your partner a copy of this piece of writing and a marker. I want you to practice being editors, thinking about the jobs that editors do," Abby referred to chart. "If you find spelling mistakes, fix them with your marker. If you think the piece needs more detail, mark a D where you think the writer should expand. If you think it doesn't make sense, be ready to talk about why."

Soon everyone was productively at work. "Children, may I stop you? Were you able to practice being editors with that piece? Great. I think you are ready for the real thing then."

Link

Send children off to edit their writing with their partners.

"It's time to get started editing the work you want to publish with your partner. You and your partner will need to decide whose piece you'll work on first. Then you will both work together to fix up that person's piece."

Notice that in this Active Involvement, children don't describe what they saw Abby do when she edited. Instead, they try their hands at doing what she demonstrated. This is a vastly preferable form of active involvement.

There will be instances such as this in which it works the best to give children actual papers to hold rather than expecting them to work off a shared text at the easel.

Don't feel like you need to elicit their suggestions. You gave them a few minutes to practice acting as editors. That's enough, now send them off to do the job!

TIME TO CONFER

Your minilesson will have set children up to reread, revise, and edit (or fix up) their writing. In conferences, watch how your children try to reread a piece they wrote earlier. You'll probably want to coach into this rereading just as you coach into children's reading. "Point under the words," you'll say. "Did that match? Try again. Point under the words and just read what you see on the page." If you can get children to reread their writing with one-to-one matching, the act of doing this will reveal places where they left out a word, deleted a word ending, need end punctuation, and so on. Encourage partners to try their hand at reading each others' writing because this, too, can reveal instances where the actual draft doesn't live up to the writer's hopes for it.

These conferences in *The Conferring Handbook* may be especially helpful today:

▶ *Conferences in part three*

Also, if you have *Conferring with Primary Writers*, you may want to refer to the conferences in part three.

Tell your children that not only do writers edit their work, they also prepare it for publication. Tell them to take some time to do this.

"Writers, you and your editors have done some nice work fixing up your pieces. Before our celebration, you are also going to want to fancy up your writing. You'll have to decide how to make your writing beautiful. Some of you may want to add colors to your cover or make your favorite page more beautiful. Decide what you could do to dress up—fancy up—your writing. And then do it!"

READING ALOUD FOR VISITORS: AN AUTHOR'S CELEBRATION

GETTING READY

▶ Page for comments attached to the back of each child's writing with the title of the piece at the top of the page

● See CD-ROM for resources

EVERY UNIT ENDS WITH CHILDREN PUBLISHING *their writing and sending it out into the world. Sometimes these are big celebrations with families and food. Other times writing celebrations might be simple occasions in which writers read their writing to each other. For this unit, Abby and I felt that the writers needed to read their stories aloud to appreciative listeners. Abby's school has reading buddies; an upper-grade class is paired with each of the lower-grade classes at P.S. 116, and the children meet once a week to read together in buddies. We decided to celebrate the stories by arranging for Abby's children to read their stories to their reading buddies.*

In this celebration, children will read their stories aloud to their reading buddies. The older children will write comments in response, and all the writers as a class will receive a big round of applause.

THE CELEBRATION

Have children sit with their published books alongside an empty chair, ready for their older buddies.

Abby's room was filled with energy and pride as the children anticipated the celebration of their writing. Each child had his or her book, and sat in his or her regular writing spot, with a chair nearby for the designated listeners who'd soon arrive. The kindergartners knew their listeners, for once a week since the start of the year each kindergartner had met with his or her fourth-grade buddy. The door opened, the fourth graders came in, and each joined his or her young partner. When there was a book buddy seated beside each kindergartener, Abby began the celebration.

Open the celebration. Describe the work your writers have done.

"Writers small and big, welcome to K–219's writing celebration! We learned to catch the Small Moments from our lives and to write about them. We took these Small Moments and stretched them long in our writing. You wrote these moments with so many details that any reader can get a really clear picture of the story. Give yourselves a pat on the back!"

All of Abby's students proceeded to raise one arm behind their heads and pat their own backs.

Ask writers to read to their buddies. Ask the buddies to listen, compliment, and write a response.

"Writers and friends, we are going to celebrate this wonderful writing by having each writer read his or her piece to his or her book buddy. Book buddy, your job is to be a good listener and then tell the writer what you liked about his or her writing. You may also ask a question. Once you tell the writer what you liked, you may write your comment on the sheet that is attached to the back of the piece of writing. You may start."

Children already know how to share texts by sitting hip to hip and listening as each other reads. They read in this fashion with their reading partners during the reading workshop.

Do this opening of the celebration in a formal way. Make this into a special occasion.

Notice that in this celebration, there is no pressure to stand at the front of the room and perform. Abby's children are kindergartners and many of them find it challenging to read even the writing they've written themselves. This intimate, supportive buddy-work is vastly more appropriate than an occasion that requires children to perform.

Soon the young writers were deeply involved in reading their stories aloud. Now the older buddies listened by leaning close to the writers and by responding. Then the buddies gave oral and written compliments. They were skilled at noticing details and quick to give their youngsters congratulatory hand shakes.

Close the ceremony by explaining to children what will happen to their piece of writing after this, inviting a round of applause, and thanking everyone.

As the reading and talking subsided, Abby told the children that their pieces of writing would be copied so that one copy could go home to be shared with families while the original published work could be hung up on the outside bulletin board for the whole world to read.

We concluded the celebration by giving the youngsters a big, loud round of applause while the writers stood and bowed proudly.

"Thank you, book buddies, for celebrating our hard work with us. Congratulations, kindergartners, for writing the stories from your lives in such magical ways."

The older book buddies, of course, are prepped ahead of time for their role.

When teachers at our summer institutes receive written responses from each other about their writing, they cherish those responses. These little love-notes matter a huge amount. Don't take them lightly.

DATE DUE
